KILL MY FEAR

SAMUEL LINTON

GLINT PUBLICATIONS

CONTENTS

Panic Attack Help	v
Introduction	vii

PART I
ONLY TWO CHOICES

1. How Did You Get Here?	3
2. The Choice Is Yours	16

PART II
KNOW YOUR ENEMY

3. The Monster In The Science Lab	45
4. Find The "Me" In Enemy	54
5. Spiritual Warfare Bootcamp	69
6. Tools Of The Torturer	78

PART III
MURDER WEAPONS

7. Getting Battle-Ready	111
8. Weapon #1: Write What's Right	116
9. Weapon #2: Walk Down What If Avenue	146
10. Weapon #3: Talk To Fear More	158

PART IV
DEAL THE DEATH BLOW

11. Make Your Move	169
12. Advance More Than Once	181

Afterword	195
Attack Panic Back	201
Can You Help Me?	203

Acknowledgments	205

SUMMARY, SCRIPTURES, AND QUESTIONS

Only Two Choices Summary	209
Know Your Enemy Summary	213
Murder Weapons Summary	219
Deal The Death Blow Summary	225
About Sam	229

PANIC ATTACK HELP

This book deals extensively destroying anxiety's grip on your life. We understand that anxiety manifests itself in many ways. One of those avenues is through panic attacks.

If you suffer from panic attacks regularly, please read through to the end of the book, and just for signing up to my mailing list, I'll give you a copy of my exclusive guide *Attack Panic Back.*

It's short, practical, and funny—like me.

But I'm really not short. Don't forget to check it out at the end.

INTRODUCTION
NINETEEN STEPS TO HELL

"Avoiding danger is no safer in the long run than outright exposure. The fearful are caught as often as the bold."

— HELEN KELLER

When a special place becomes an evil place, it does so unexpectedly.

That special place doesn't announce, "Hey I'm going to grow fangs and bite you in the carotid!"

It didn't send me a Facebook message.

The back room behind our sanctuary we've always coined as the "Secret Place," a place of last-minute prayer before sermons, jokes with the worship team, and occasionally some awesome stories.

For instance, a woman was about to be

baptized. While approaching the tank, she conceived the thought that baptism just isn't legit unless you go commando. Nonchalantly, like she was passing the ketchup, she handed her unmentionables to the pastor right before he baptized her. Fun times!

You thought ministry was all G-Rated, didn't you?

But this night was different.

I stood downstairs in the kitchen of our church. There is a narrow, private stairwell which leads up to the SP (Secret Place, for those of you not paying attention), and I was there when one of the baptismal administrators called down the steps. "Pastor Sam! You're up right after this song."

I can't recall exactly what I was doing down in the kitchen. I'd like to paint a picture that it was something noble like praying for someone's lost three-legged dog, or saving a marriage, or leading seventeen bikers to Christ, but cookie dough is probably the number one "what the survey said" likely answer. I was probably eating raw cookie dough (because it's in the fridge, and also because do you even need a second reason). I know it's for visitors, but come on! You would have been right there next to me searching for a plastic spoon like the Ark of the Covenant.

Whatever I was doing, I don't recall.

When he said that, I looked up the steps and saw

the six baptismal candidates waiting for me to baptize them.

And everything happened in slow motion, but all at once.

I couldn't breathe.

I couldn't think.

I couldn't speak.

I was frozen.

As the band wrapped up the final repeat of a familiar worship song, I plummeted into a dark and foreign place. This is a place that I would know all too well in the days ahead.

I was having a full-blown panic attack. I summoned every bit of my strength to walk the steps up to the landing where the baptismal coordinator stood waiting. When I reached the top step, my lung capacity was so restricted that I could hardly form a sentence.

I grabbed the volunteer and said, "Tell the band to play the next song. I... can't... do this. I'm late."

"Next song—I—they're stopping now, Pastor Sam."

The last note was played, the baptismal candidates were only slightly aware of my presence, but all I could do was plead once more for our team to spontaneously reconfigure the order of a two-hundred-person worship service.

The coordinator ran out to the sanctuary proper. And amid the silence I heard him say to the worship leader who was only slightly audible from my vantage point, "Go on, we aren't ready."

The worship leader, way quicker on his feet than I was, jumped into the final song throwing the musicians and production team into chaos.

I grabbed the coordinator's arm and said, "Please pray for me, please. I'm having a panic attack."

I remember the words coming out of my mouth as slow as sludge. It took every effort to form a coherent thought as I raced to find my breath and my eloquence at the same time. Again, tension coiled around my lungs, restricting my air flow. I felt three hundred pounds heavier (insert cookie-dough callback here).

Somehow, I managed to put on my game face to baptize the people. We laughed, joked, and I baptized all of them without incident. As soon as I said the last amen, the worship leader began a thirty second prayer, giving me the gap that I needed to get to the platform.

It was nineteen steps to the platform and I didn't make it.

Nineteen steps.

Panic seized every part of me. I came out as the worship leader was praying about everything to fill the vacant pastor-less space (the Steelers, the sun shining to melt the Pittsburgh snow, oxygen, that the cookie dough would be intact to deliver fresh baked cookies for visitors). He was praying for anything and everything to give me time to take my place.

I could not take the remaining five steps up to the platform. I grabbed one of the band members sitting in the front of the congregation and handed him my list of announcements, begging him to read them because I was having another panic attack. He gaped at me, stunned, but also incredibly unnerved. He didn't have a microphone or a clue what to announce.

From the corner of my eye, I could see the worship leader glaring down at me as I stood trembling with both of my arms on the band member who was "off that night."

As before, I managed to compose myself, take the extra five steps to the platform, and deliver the three-minute announcements.

As I exited the stage, I felt like I had the flu. My mouth was dry, my head was pounding, and every muscle in my body ached like I had completed the entire P90X program in ten minutes. I stumbled into the vestibule as the other pastor began preaching the sermon. The worship team was surrounding the baptismal coordinator as he recounted his version of the events. He stopped talking when he saw me.

A picture formed in my mind of moments before where the embellished story entertained the worship team. "Dude [which I'm certain he said], he seriously just wet himself back there. Not only that, I had to wrestle the cookie dough out of his hand just to get him to go to the platform."

Laugh, laugh. Chuckle, chuckle. "Yeah, our pastor is cray cray!"

At least, that's how I imagined it.

The band member who was off came out of the sanctuary behind me and asked if I was okay. The worship leader looked shocked. Instrumentalists and vocalists alike stood in silence.

I felt like a bad science experiment. Not like the cool volcano that the third grader made whose dad happened to be an engineer. You know, the volcano that had its own engine in it? But the one that was basically just play-dough with a hole in the top containing an Alka Seltzer tablet.

Total train wreck.

I could only say one thing—one thing. And I'd repeat this thought over and over again for months until I got a clue of what was going on.

"I'm so sorry."

"I'm really sorry," I repeated, almost in tears, "I'm really embarrassed."

The baptismal coordinator broke the silence and made the statement that would haunt me for an entire year.

"Well, don't do that again! Because if something like that happens to you, what does that mean for the rest of us?"

He was right. I'm the leader. I'm the pastor. I am

spiritually mature. Why wasn't I more selfless? Why wasn't I more spiritual? How could I let something so routine wreck me?

After all, this wasn't my first rodeo. I'd walked those steps thousands of times. I'd been a pastor for twelve years!

How?

How could this be happening...to ME?

I abdicated my duties of the closing announcements with such a wave of relief. I felt great knowing that I didn't have to do this anymore (I'll explain later why this was the first and maybe even the worst mistake I made).

It lasted two minutes. That peaceful ease was replaced with a reverberating question.

What if this happens again?

There were three more services that weekend that I was responsible for announcements. That represented six (opening and closing) places where I could have a pan—

Nah! Shut up. Who cares? It's just three minutes.

That persistent question gave way to another question:

What if this happens when I'm preaching a thirty-minute sermon? What if this happens...next weekend when I preach?

Though I'm not a professional boxer, I would compare the feeling I had leaving the church to just finishing ten rounds with Mike Tyson (both of my ears now bitten off) and a darkness flooded over me that words fail to define.

The word that most aptly fit the situation was *dread*.

In six days, I would have to stand up and teach the Bible to the church for thirty minutes. Four times in a row.

Well, don't do that again! Because if something like that happens to you, what does that mean for the rest of us. Those words pierced my inner monologue.

I was kicking off a brand new series that we had been advertising since before Christmas.

It won't happen again, right? I mean, it's out of my system?

But what if this DOES happen when I'm preaching? Hundreds and hundreds of people will see.

No, it's just a fluke, I assured myself.

Only it wasn't.

When Did Fear Move In?

How did your battle with fear and anxiety start? When did you have your first panic attack? Was it in a crowd of people? Was it alone in your car? Was it during a fight with your spouse? Was it when you woke up from a dream?

Was it when you were told about that sickness? Perhaps when you were given information about someone you loved.

Newsflash: it doesn't have to be particularly dramatic. Mine wasn't. I was late going up to baptize some people. Big deal! I've preached to hundreds of people. I'm responsible for a large and growing church in the process of a ten-million- dollar building project.

But still, here I was. And still, here you are.

Fighting fear doesn't have to make sense.

But sometimes, fear calls us out to the playground for a fight. And my call came on a snowy January evening when I was doing something so routine.

What fear wakes you at night and keeps you from sleep? What event do you replay over and over causing you to lose your breath?

You have to have one, or you would have passed this book up. You would have said, "Fear? Me? No way. I'm going to go read that latest *Star Wars* story because fear for me took place a long time ago in a galaxy far away."

But I know you're struggling if you're reading this.

Since I began speaking openly about my experience with anxiety, I became quickly aware that my situation in that backroom was not abnormal. It was typical. This gave me a great realization. It took me so long to accept and embrace this truth. But I want to share it with you now to save you time, maybe even years.

I'm not alone. And neither are you.

This is the book that I needed someone to give me the night I had that panic attack. This is the book that would have given me hope and camaraderie. I didn't have it, and I had to stumble into all of these truths on my own without clear direction, having only God's grace to guide me into momentary respites of peace.

But I want to give it to you. Because if God can offer me a way to come through this, there is hope for any who would move forward.

I wish this book wasn't so long. I'm not an environmentalist or anything, but I wish you didn't have to read and think so much about this stuff in order to get out from under it. The trees would be happy, too. Probably not Bob Ross happy, but happy, still.

There is no magic bullet for chronic fear or anxiety.

That's the number one question others ask me.

That's not to say that this journey will last the rest of your life. However, there is no instant fix. Not even a little bit. I'd love to be the infomercial host speaking to you during your sleepless, anxiety-ridden night offering you the cure for $9.99.

That'll never happen.

For starters, I'd never look good that late at night. As the day goes on, my good looks are challenged by the elements. I'm okay with it.

The main problem, however, is that we are living

in a culture that demands results quickly. We'd even be willing to pay for it. Unfortunately, healing doesn't work that way.

I've talked to many members of the church about my battle with chronic anxiety. The one question that I've been asked repeatedly is the only one that I can't answer.

"So, what eventually got it to stop? What happened?"

I'm not sure. I don't know what it was specifically. I know everything that I did. But I'm unable to limit the healing to one activity. I do, however, have some ideas of what contributed most to my healing.

One of my most valuable lessons concerning this centers around individuality. I know that there were things that meant the world to me that certainly wouldn't have the same weight in your world. I know that the fears that I have don't match yours. I know that my spiritual exercises may seem excessive to some, and yet not extreme enough for others. But of one thing I am positive for all of us. So, let's get some solidarity around this one point, no matter where we are in our battle with anxiety and no matter what tools we want to use to combat it:

We all have to kill the crap out of fear.

Why Listen To Me?

I'm writing this to you because, well, frankly, I'm not a hoarder.

I don't believe that healing should be hoarded.

Yes, I said healing. God healed me of debilitating anxiety without my ever taking any medicine (we will explore this more later). It was far from instant, but as I am writing this, I believe it is complete. My belief about healing is that it should never terminate with the healed person. Someone like me who has been healed from anxiety should be vigilant about helping others take the God-directed steps to become free from the same bondage.

> "[God]...comforts us in all our affliction, so
> that we may be able to comfort those who
> are in any affliction, with the comfort
> with which we ourselves are comforted
> by God."
>
> — 2 Corinthians 1:3–4, ESV

Healing is possible. Heck, healing is likely. Healing is attainable. Say it any way you'd like. But until you swallow this and make it your own, you're dead in anxiety's water.

Anxiety, chronic fear, constant panic, and overwhelming dread do not have to be permeant parts of your story. I would love to tell you that these afflictions come only to slightly overweight pastors with huge personalities, but that simply isn't true. One in six people struggle with anxiety. Most remain undiagnosed with a panic disorder. Google it.

What I am going to attempt to do is help you. There are two reasons why I'm writing this to you. The first is selfish and the second is not so selfish.

First, I've always loved writing. As long as I can remember, transferring ideas from my mind to paper has been one of the most unbelievably beautiful processes I've ever experienced. That's the selfish part.

Secondly, I'm writing to you the book I needed when I took those nineteen steps. I'm writing the book that I wish someone had handed me the night I had my first panic attack. The people I've spoken with whose lives suffer under the weight of anxiety need this. Children who don't know how to live without fear need this. Anyone who has a panic attack a day needs this.

I needed this.

I want to help you. I believe that God permits us to experience things sometimes completely for the benefit of others. That's what He revealed to me when I was coming to the end of this. It was never about me, and frankly, it never will be. Regardless of how noble we think we are, we all tend to be selfish. Unfortunately, we can't easily comprehend how desperately connected to each other we are. Sometimes, God leads us to experience this connection through the bonds of affliction.

Suffering is, after all, the universal language.

I'm going to spend the remaining time in this book telling you my story and sharing what I've learned.

First, I am a Christian pastor, but you don't have to be a Christian to walk with me through this journey.

I always found it a little befuddling that there is a Christian section in the bookstore. Might I suggest something that's a little revolutionary? Either the principles that I'm outlining here work for you or they don't. It doesn't much matter what you believe.

I believe that regardless of whether you confess Jesus Christ as your Lord or not, all good things that have come into your life are a result of God permitting them. You might see otherwise, and I won't argue with you about that. But what I won't do is to say that these principles are isolated only for church folk.

Andy Stanley once gave a talk and asserted that all of the heroes of the Bible that followed Jesus spent a great deal of time initially not believing in His identity. They simply followed and listened.

There were no disciples standing at the tomb of Christ on the third day with a stopwatch counting down the moments that Jesus was going to explode from the earth and give them hope after death. He told them he would, but apparently they hadn't bought into His vision. Instead they were all going about their business trying to reconcile what happened to them. Fortunately, Jesus still loved them and eventually revealed to them His true identity. Might I suggest to you as we work through these principles that you accept my belief that God gave them to me through the power of the resurrection of Jesus Christ.

Another quick bit of housekeeping: I have an odd sense of humor. It's not a coping mechanism, it's me. It's like having brown eyes or freckles. Not that either of those things is bad. I've been told I joke a lot in the pulpit, and some like that—and others simply just need to go repent for being sinfully straightforward. Just kidding to all you serious brothers and sisters. Loooooooove you!

But seriously, learning to laugh is one of God's greatest healing strategies, in my humble opinion.

Speaking of humble opinions, picture the worst doctor you know. Got him in your mind? He hasn't invested in a new white coat since graduating from medical school right when Reagan brought the Wall down. On top of that, his hair is disheveled, and you get the impression he likes to binge weird shows on Netflix during operations. Not even like *Stranger Things*, but some of the ones that only received a One-Star review. Got him in your mind? Good.

I'm still not as qualified as him to talk about the medical and psychological effects of anxiety disorder with 100% authority. I'm not a doctor. I'm not a medical professional. I'm not even really smart. I'm similar to Dr. Phil with less insight and about a hundred million less dollars.

But I know panic attacks. I got street cred, son. So when I speak, give me an ear. I promise there's something in my messy message that might help you, but I need your attention. Because I'm about to share with you the most important decision that you have to make concerning panic, anxiety, and constant fear. Don't worry, there are only two options. Now, grab your cookie dough, and a notebook. This is gonna get bumpy.

How Kill My Fear Works

Let's clear the decks and talk about how this is going to work. *Kill My Fear* may not be conventional like many other books on anxiety. It's short, by design.

First, we are going to talk about the only two options we have for dealing with fear and crippling anxiety. Yeah, we aren't going to go over every phobia, mood disorder, bad thinking pattern, etc. There are tons of others more qualified to do that.

Instead, you and I are going to have the conversation that begins, "Okay, so, now what?" That's where this book really starts. I'm going to assume you struggle with anxiety to some level, or else you probably would have picked up the latest book by James Patterson or Stephen King. Or, if you're like me, you picked up both!

Secondly, we are going to do a deep dive on the most common tactics of how fear is at work in your life. Again, we aren't going to go into the specifics so much as the most common overarching ways that fear attacks our minds and our spiritual lives.

Third, we are going to switch to offense. I'm going to furnish you with some tools (at least the ones that I know how to use) to see immediate and lasting results dealing with fear. How can we kill fear if we come to a Gladiator-style batter armed with bubble gum? Nah, we need to open the weapons chest and get a little medieval on fear.

Finally, we are going to close it out with the ultimate way to ensure we eliminate debilitating anxiety for good. That's a bold reach, but I promise you, it's possible. I say that because I've done it. Am I perfect with it? Negative, Ghost Rider, but I am scores better at handling fear than I was before my battle with fear began.

So, that's all.

Oh, I almost forgot. Because it's 2020 and you probably are reading this while seeing what's going on with Trump, what's happening with the Kardashians, while Instagramming your favorite meal, and keeping your Snapchat streak alive, I'm going to include a TL;DR (Too Long; Didn't Read—or Summary, if you prefer) section at the end of the book. It's going to be short enough that you can catch it in between tweets. It'll also include some discussion questions that might help you process what we are talking about.

So, yeah, that's really all. Let's jump in the tank and get ready to ride against fear.

PART I

ONLY TWO CHOICES

"Inaction breeds doubt and fear. Action breeds confidence and courage. If you want to conquer fear, do not sit home and think about it. Go out and get busy."

— DALE CARNEGIE

1
HOW DID YOU GET HERE?

Considering myself a fairly confident person, the idea of paralyzing anxiety was as far removed from me as going to a bakery and ordering only skim milk. Not gonna happen.

But there I was, Sunday evening, sitting in this wrecked home that was my mind. Up to this point, it was moderately decorated with positive thoughts of upcoming public speaking opportunities and experience with ministry.

But now it was a dark room.

I pictured a living room fancily decorated. It was the kind of room requiring you to remove your shoes before entering. The carpet was perfectly cleaned.

Then, the scene changed. A dark cloak fell across this room, muting the lighting. There was an unmistakable smell of "former."

Former days of confidence.
Former good times.
Former light.

All the former was replaced with a darkness and instability. The furniture was soiled, the curtains shredded, the carpet mauled: evidence of a struggle against fear and its subsequent victory.

I hoped no one would knock on this door. They'd surely be ashamed I'm living in here. Especially because they remembered what it was like just a week ago. It originally was like a Febreze commercial; now it looked like the backdrop of the thirtieth sequel to the movie *Saw*.

Relief from the weekend's anxiety attacks didn't come. The reason was simple. Sunday was on its way. I checked the flight board, and it was on time.

And the moment the church service ended, though the immediate tension of panic was gone, what remained was sheer foreboding and dread.

I believe my mental scenario is not at all unique. When you struggle with fear, it redecorates the walls in your mind. I felt this overwhelming feeling of loss and despair because I couldn't do what I was used to doing. I began to go into mourning over the person I once was.

Your former identity is collateral damage to fear. It's not at all surprising that many that struggle with anxiety also struggle with depression. It's because, like me, you're grieving. You're grieving the loss of yourself. You're grieving the loss of a former ability or dream that has since evacuated from your life.

But that's why understanding your power in this battle is so vital, and that's where you can truly redecorate your mind with shades of victory again. But it's going to come back to only two choices.

The Sermon That Almost Ended Me

I practiced in in front of a mirror. I memorized the key points and illustrations. I had it color-coded and ready to go in my Bible. But the amount of preparation I had done didn't solve the greatest problem that I had the following day.

What's going to happen to the nineteen steps.

This lesson about anxiety didn't hit me until way after. I think we really go after the symptoms and things that we can control, but we cower away from working on the things that will make the biggest difference. That's how I was with preparation for the sermon.

Believe it or not, I practiced. I actually walked up and down my steps at home several times. I pretended to be in a hurry and I arrived to the second floor without being winded.

But as soon as I thought about the nineteen steps from stairwell to pulpit, my breath and concentration failed and I felt more exasperated than a vegan in a Big Mac eating competition. Not pretty and not even close to being logical.

The time came where I was set to deliver the sermon. I arrived two hours early to the sanctuary, completely dressed and ready for preaching. I sat on the baptismal steps, overlooking my nineteen steps and listened as the band rehearsed, working through the music and fine tuning it.

This is the music that is going to transition you into failure. (My inner voice said.)

These are the steps that that will end your career.

Do those shoes go with this outfit?

I thought that kind of stuff too, because quite frankly it's way better to have a psychological meltdown if your outfit matches with your shoes.

Oh, look at that loser. It's one thing that he lost his mind and is drooling, but he didn't even bother to match his socks to his outfit! What a farce!

My boss, Mike called to check on me.

"Are you feeling like you'll be okay?"

"Yeah, I'm good. Just a little freaked." I felt like sobbing. I hadn't realized one of those huge tears had formed and slowly traveled down my cheek. You know the ones. You can see the reflection in them from across the room. It was about the size of a small snow globe.

"You're not good, are you?"

"I'm really not." I breathed out thinking of ninety

minutes later how breath would be everything to me.

"Sam, this is evil. This is an attack. It's all that it is. You're gonna do good."

"I just [breath began to leave at this point] don't know how—I can do this."

"If you have an attack up there, just step to the side and wait until you're composed."

How ludicrous. I don't know when it subsides. I have no clue.

"Okay. It'll be okay," I assured him. I felt horrible knowing I was putting this pressure on him. He was having me preach and here I am, requiring him to turn into a coach just to get me to get off the back steps.

"I'll be there if something goes really wrong, but don't worry."

Whatever I was feeling was far from worry. It was something altogether in another county, and it was paralyzing me.

T-minus thirty minutes.

I sat in the back gripping my Bible, and a water. I hadn't had anything to eat or drink all day and I was lightheaded.

Prior to this, my caffeine intake had been between a sixty-four gallon Sunoco drum and greater. Because I had caffeine the day of the panic attack, I assumed it was a contributor.

I was wrong.

The time went slow and fast all at once. As I opened my notes and examined my first memorized point, my breath would evacuate quicker than George Costanza did during that apartment fire with the kids and senior citizens (Google it).

Pastor Ron, the other minister that I work with, came up. I expected him to tell me he was worried. I expected him to tell me that he'd preach for me. I hoped that he'd tell me that I could have the night off, but it turns out, he was one of the first people that spoke something to me that I desperately needed to hear.

"Go ahead, just go you're fine."

I'm fine, I thought. Do you hear me wheezing? I mean, seriously. I can't even form a thought let alone captivate an audience for thirty minutes.

"You're fine," he said, rather flatly. "It's gonna be fine. Nothing is going to happen to you. Mike and I will be here, but you're not going to need us."

"I'm not fine, this is wrong. It's getting worse." I was saying this, unconsciously praying that someone would step in and force me to leave.

"It's going to be good, nothing is wrong. You're good at this, you got this."

That pep talk was so important.

I don't want to wait to tell you why. Panic, anxiety, stress, depression, all come at us with an exit strategy planned. They want you out, bottom line. It's far beyond even what you imagine.

They want you to stop disciplining your kids. They want you to quit your job. They want you to take the moral low ground to accommodate those around you. They want you to not take that trip you had planned.

All that to say this: the people in your life that are challenging you to stay on course are the good guys. Period. Full stop.

Pastor Ron finished pep talking, the band finished playing, and I was in agony still.

I wish that I could accurately describe it. Time wouldn't permit. But I felt like I was in a vacuum of hopelessness—a cauldron of incalculable despair. I felt heavy and completely weightless all at once. But one recurring thought reverberated through the depths of my being.

I'm not going to make it. I'm late. I'm not going to make it.

The third song of the four-song set blared over the sound system of the worshipping church. My mind played out every bad scenario.

They'll laugh at me. The visitors that came tonight to hear the Gospel will never return.

I'll lose my job.

My pregnant wife will be all alone because I'll be the one needing care, in a mental institution—which is where I deserved to go. Because sane people don't do a job for twelve years and all of sudden have a heart-wrenching paralyzing fear while doing it.

That's not what sane people do.

These thoughts and others rattled the cage of my subconscious like a hungry lion at the San Diego zoo.

The last song expired, and the announcements and a twenty second opening video stood between me and this new horror, this new level of fresh hell that had become my life.

I took my nineteen steps into it.

Like A Stinky, Twenty Year-Old Car

One of the best cars that I owned was a 1995 Honda Accord. I bought it in 2008, because I'm into vintage. I also didn't have money. So there's that.

The car looked beautiful on the outside. It was black with tinted windows and a moonroof. I'm a sucker for a moonroof. I bought the car at the bitter end of November, and I remember buttoning up my coat after having the title transferred because of how cold it was.

I sat inside the car and thought, *well, I've never owned a car with a moonroof.* I checked the temperature on my phone. It was a balmy forty-one degrees. Rationalization kicked in and I thought, *well, I have a coat on. Why would I waste a perfectly good moonroof opportunity? Isn't this what all moonroof owners do?*

So, there I was, coasting down the highway with a moonroof back and my system up! But the honeymoon lasted for about two minutes. I realized there were some definite problems with the car. When I got home, I made a very detailed list:

- Front leather interior was ripping (meaning, the tears were so large in the seats you could use them for storage). No problem. I'll order a couple new seats when I save up some money.
- The car smelled like it was an ashtray. I'm not talking about a vape ashtray (are there vape ashtrays?). I mean a legit, 1970s bingo hall ashtray. Seriously, before the smoking ban, did you ever walk into a bingo hall? How could they see the numbers through the smoke? No biggie. I'd get it detailed.
- The window rolled down on the driver's side, but it didn't go up well. And when I say that, I mean it went up about fifty percent of the time. Sometimes you had to smash the door on the inside to get the mechanism to work, not too much, just until your hand hurt. Again, when I get the interior detailed, maybe I'll have them get a new motor for that window.
- The odometer read 171,000 miles. And it

> never went up once in the five years that I owned the car. It was a miracle car that didn't age. It was like Benjamin Button. (Well, I guess he aged in reverse.)

This was the short list of things I was planning on taking care of *immediately*. A week turned into a month. A month turned into a year. And before I knew it, when people would ride in the car with me, I'd have to give them the run-own of every problem to mentally prepare them for the trip. Meanwhile, I'd become accustomed to the rusty ageless time machine with the sick moonroof.

I got used to those things.

But an outsider might say, "Yikes, dude! Fix the window. At least get the inside detailed better so you don't smell like the Marlboro Man's underwear drawer."

And I would make that outsider leave my car because frankly, I don't have the time for that type of negativity.

We are like this with life. We get used to things. Things at first shock us. Then they annoy us. Pretty soon, they don't even faze us. And that's most of our problems. We do that with cars, relationships, work situations, financial situations, marital connections.

And we do it with fear.

Come on! You know the person.

They won't go outside at night because they've

gotten used to a fear that they'll be hurt. They won't ride in a car because they've become accustomed to the fact that it's easier to be home instead of risking being in an accident. They won't go online and sign up for a dating profile because they're afraid of getting hurt. It's easier to be alone. They avoid that difficult conversation, because they're afraid of the rejection that person will make them feel if they truly reveal their feelings about an unhealthy situation.

At first, living this way is like eating three bags of marshmallows -- cray cray. But then, it becomes a regular conversation.

"I don't_____(insert activity you avoid) because I'm afraid of _____(insert potential negative outcome)."

Everyone stands and looks and says, "Dude, how are you okay with this? Why don't you change?"

But truthfully, you've forgotten what an opportunity to break free looks like.

How Quickly Normal Changes

Despite how long I've worked in ministry and how many people I've encountered, I suppose one of those mic-dropping lessons that I never get used to is this:

Anyone's life can change overnight.

This happens so frequently that we think every time it occurs, it's an exception. It's actually the rule.

Your life is going to change.

Something good and something bad is going to change it.

It could be something amazing or something cataclysmic.

You read your wife's text messages and you will never look at her the same after you saw the way she talked to another man.

You heard the doctor say the C word and your name in the same sentence.

You held the hand of a loved one that passed -- that promised they'd be with you forever.

I've realized it helps to view life through the scope of seasons. Because there is no certainty that things will last. Some seasons are very, very, very, very long. Like the credits to a Marvel movie at the end when you await the after-teaser for the following movie.

Seriously, they go on forever. Come on, just let me know what Tony Stark is going to do in the Marvel universe so I can go pee!

I needed to preach this to myself when I entered this season, but I didn't, I simply didn't.

I did what most of us do.

Assume that this season is going to last forever.

This is gonna be my normal. Huffing and puffing

into the platform, pleading for prayer and agonizing over nineteen freaking steps. This is my new forever normal.

What a lie.

What a scam.

2

THE CHOICE IS YOURS

Back to the story.

I ended up preaching the sermon.

That weekend. I nailed it. I mean that in the most God-honoring way. It was well-received. I left it all on the platform. I felt that God himself came down and took my weakness and set me aside, and allowed Himself to work through me.

And I won. It was over. I conquered it.

But I didn't.

That's not even close to true at all. I thought I did. I thought that it would be over. Until the following week, when I went up to perform the announcements, two minutes, five items, nothing compared to the thirty minutes from the previous week.

I experienced a massive panic attack. The same as I had before.

It was only just beginning.

Pastor Steven Furtick said once that God's reward for winning a big battle is usually another battle. The weekend of the first sermon after the panic attack would turn out to be one of the easiest during my war with anxiety.

But that's kind of your story, too, isn't it? I mean, you thought it was over and you'd won, only to find yourself in the same boat.

You thought fear was an isolated sales person that came to your door that you had to shoo away, but as it turned out, they moved their belongings into your bedroom, and when you went to go to sleep you found them in your bed! They followed you to work. They even changed the presets on your car radio! When you opened your phone, fear made its picture your home screen and lock screen. So clever!

Fear has invaded every bit of you.

Choice 1: Run From Fear, And Accommodate It

What I'm about to say may be different than other wisdom written in books about fear. There is an abundance of resources out there to help you *manage fear*.

This book isn't one of them. I'm not going to write about strategies to cope and different ways to move into a life lived with anxiety. That's why I must be honest from the get-go, to give you an opportunity to return this title and pick up something by a preacher with more letters behind his name!

You see, there aren't a ton of choices on how to deal with fear. There are only two, in my estimation. Let's examine choice one, a choice that a solid percentage of our anxiety-ridden population has made.

Choice 1: You can run from fear, and accommodate it.

Yes, this is a choice. You may say, "Wow dude, that's savage. How can you say that people are running from fear and accommodating it?"

I will answer your question with another.

How many words do you know with phobia in the title?

Go ahead.

Count.

You know at least four, I know it. Come on, you know arachnohobia (fear of spiders), agoraphobia (fear of open or crowded places), claustrophobia (fear of enclosed spaces), hydrophobia (fear of water).

But did you know that there are way more than that!

Let's go through some uncommon ones:

- Nomophobia—fear of not having mobile phone access. This is the newest way to

punish teenagers. Control the device and you control the child. I think that was in Proverbs.
- Ablutophobia—fear of washing or bathing. I think it's safe to say this fear stinks.
- Linonophobia—fear of string. People that struggle with that fear are barely hanging on by a thread.

I should stop this.

Now, knowing this, let's talk about how we accommodate said fears.

Oh, I've always wanted to go on an Alaskan cruise. I spend my free time at work Googling images of that beautiful wilderness and how great it would be to see all those wonderful wild animals [note: I don't know what people get excited about specifically with regards to Alaskan cruises]. *I would go on one, but I have hydrophobia. I am terrified of water. So for now, these beautiful images of Alaska will have to do. I mean, after all, I don't NEED to go on a cruise.*

Or...

I have a big job interview on that corner office on the 32nd floor of the skyscraper. It's my dream job. The only problem is, I am claustrophobic, I'm afraid of elevators. It's only sixty-four flights of stairs to the top. Hey, I'll just pack gym clothes to the interview. They'll hire me because they'll see how in shape I am and how my sweat *smells like strawberries when I get to the top, huffing and puffing. But at LEAST I don't have to go in that elevator, oh wretched suspended coffin of doom.*

How about this...

I want to marry him. I really do. I know that he loves me. But my last break up was more than I could bear. I can't go through that twice. I don't want more baggage. If I don't commit, I won't have to suffer loss. This is fine what we are doing, I'm sure he'll stay with me knowing that I have one foot out the door.

Even this...

I know that my life is a mess because I was molested. I know that it shows itself in the way I relate to my wife and the way I treat my kids. I want to get help, but no one knows. If someone finds out, I'll feel dirty, ashamed, and they'll think differently of me. This is something I've dealt with all my life. I just have to learn to deal. I won't understand true intimacy with my spouse, but I'll care for them and love them as best as I know how.

Shall I stop? What's yours? How have you accommodated it?

Because that's what we have to do, right? Fear comes knocking at your door, and we show it to the guest room. Before we know it, it's moved into our living room. It erases all the on-demand shows we wanted to watch! How are we going to find out what's going on with the Kardashians?

Before you know it, you're accommodating fear in your living space. You're choosing your meals based on fear's dietary restrictions. Fear is gluten-free and it destroys Pizza Friday. Fear is lactose intolerant and the milkshakes you and your daughter make together give fear gas.

You get the gist?

But you have accommodated fear. You have figured out ways to work around it. And you've become very creative.

This is where you might say, okay, but those things happened to me, I was a victim. I was hurt.

I agree with you, trust me. In fact, I sympathize with you. I have counseled hundreds of people whose lives have been derailed by things and people beyond their control. And it wasn't their choice. It couldn't have been avoided.

Fearful situations cannot be avoided. However, living with fear dominating your life can.

So my question is this:

When did you make that choice to live in fear? I'm not asking what the fearful circumstance was that you reverted to, I'm asking when did you allow living in fear to become your way of living?

Goliath Like You've Never Seen Him

So, we've covered choice Number One. Now, let's take a look at an example from the Bible before we explore Option Deux.

David and Goliath.

We are going to keep going back to this, and I promise, unlike every other Bible story, we aren't going to focus on David getting the victory. I mean, of course, a little bit we will. I am a preacher, that story is preacher gold! But we really need to examine the character that doesn't get nearly as much air time.

Goliath.

Yeah, I am sympathizing with Goliath. No one ever has a t-shirt of Goliath. No one ever tweets about Goliath.

But Goliath represents fear. He represents what we are avoiding.

> "And there came out from the camp of the Philistines a champion named Goliath of Gath, whose height was six cubits and a span. He had a helmet of bronze on his head, and he was armed with a coat of mail, and the weight of the coat was five thousand shekels of bronze."
>
> — 1 Samuel 17:4–5, ESV

Goliath is big and he's formidable. He is not just a guy that you could probably take in a fight. He's a guy that will invariably kill you. And that's why the Philistines put him in that position. He inspires fear.

Here is the truth about fear: no matter what

anyone tells you, it's scary what you're going through.

I know you've had well-meaning friends say, "Oh come on, you're being silly. God is bigger than that. You worry too much." I know that that kind of talk has only served to shame you. And I'm not going to do that.

Let's acknowledge what others won't. This fear is bigger than you can handle. It's not an issue of faith, it's an issue of your perspective. And right now, your perspective says that you are facing a nine-foot-tall giant that takes everything from you.

> "When Saul and all Israel heard these words of the Philistine, they were dismayed and greatly afraid."
>
> — 1 Samuel 17:11, ESV

No kidding.

This monster comes out, and speaks venomous fearful statements for over a month. And the Israelites remain.

It becomes a part of who they are. It becomes a part of their story. And that's what's happened to you. You saw a Goliath. You saw a formidable obstacle, and you have frozen. Life has now been you trying to avoid Goliath at all costs.

Can you still have joy in life? Sure! I'd imagine

there were some awesome conversations happening when the Israelites were encamped hiding from Goliath. Maybe they started some cool games. Maybe this is where Pogs came from. They sat on that hill and had some tournaments (Google Pogs, young ones).

But do you believe that this is what your life should be? Do you believe that you're supposed to choose stepping around Goliath forever, making sure that when you wake up that you don't do anything that's going to cause Goliath to lunge at you? Do you believe that fear will one day become a good bunk mate for you, your spouse, your children and your friends?

If so, then like the majority of Israel, choose the first option. Choice One. Go pick up some of those books that teach you how to make friends with phobias. Try to get out of anything that keeps you from facing what's in the valley waiting for you.

I know that I'm talking about. I did the same thing.

Wedding Blues

One of the longest weeks of my life was the week after my initial panic attack. The only advantage was that I finished preparing my upcoming sermon on Tuesday (unheard of) because I was so worried about not being ready. Remember, I wasn't ready for the baptismal candidates. Therefore, being "ready" became my anxiety anthem (we'll learn more about that in the "Tools of the Torturer" section).

Adding to the pressure of preaching that weekend, one of my best friends, the son of the other pastor (my boss) was getting married. Praise be to God on high I wasn't performing the wedding. However, I was to do the opening toast/benediction over the meal at the reception. It was a two-minute speaking job, at most. At a wedding reception, anything keeping you from eating is essentially the worst thing you've ever encountered. You already wait an hour or two for the bride and groom to get there. Then, someone grabs a microphone and works on their amateur stand-up comedy routine.

"Oh, look! That guy is juggling! That's awesome, now give me my $75 rubbery chicken meal and cake so I can blow this popsicle stand." I'm sorry, I've been involved in a lot of weddings.

The day of the wedding, I made two terrible mistakes.

First, I didn't acknowledge the foreboding and pain going on inside of me. Outwardly, I was giddy, gregarious, and fun-loving. If people around me had seen me from the inside, it would have looked like I had grown a second head, with bad breath and a large nose ring.

I was a mess.

Like a hundred miles south of messed up.

But Moses wasn't the only one who had to deal with De-Nile (corny church humor), I didn't acknowledge it.

To anyone. Even myself.

It wasn't until one hour before the wedding that I started sweating and feeling nauseous. Thirty minutes before, I wasn't speaking to hardly anyone. Even my wife.

During the ceremony, I remember just rehearsing my prayer (two minutes max) in my mind. And as we processed down to the connected reception hall, it started all over again: tightness in my chest, sweating, shortness of breath.

I approached the crowded reception, filled with about 150 people, most of them I knew very well over the years. The DJ said, "Hey Pastor Sam, here's your mic, you don't need help from me."

But I did. *Pray for me*, I thought. *Tell me it's going to be okay. I'm not going to do this. I can't.*

I'm going to embarrass myself.

I'm going to be the story. The story at this wedding.

I'm going to be the YouTube clip. Headline: "Pastor passes out while praying at boss's son's wedding, awakens just before cake is cut to carb load."

This is it.

But mostly, I was afraid of hurting my friend.

If this happens to you, what does that mean for the rest of us?

At that thought, a full-blown panic attack began again.

I was sitting toward the front of the crowded, wonderfully decorated venue, unable to speak. No one noticed, but my wife. She knew something was wrong. As the DJ announced the bride and groom, over the thunderous applause and cheers, I got to my feet gasping for my breath.

It didn't come. I was foggy, covered in sweat, and almost on the verge of tears.

In the time it took them to make their way to the bridal table, placed strategically on the raised platform of the aisle, I made the second mistake of that day—and one that I still regret.

I grabbed the groom's older brother.

Being my closest friend, I was extremely quick. "Tony," I shouted over the applause, "I'm having a panic attack, I can't do this, can you please open the meal in prayer?"

He looked at me with concern and care, and shame ran through me like a river of Hell.

He put his hand on my shoulder and said, "Sure, Sam, no biggie, just pray, that's it?"

"That's it," I gasped, still unable to breath regularly.

Calmly, he made his way back to the booth where the DJ was setting up to announce my name. He whispered to the DJ, the DJ announced him, and he proceeded to pray the most perfect and confident prayer ever spoken at a wedding.

When he walked back to our table, he put his arm on my shoulder once more and gave it a squeeze.

A new feeling overtook me, one that I had begun to feel comfortable wearing and one that would make its way into the permanent hard drive of my 2016 memories.

I was ashamed. I had failed. I let down my friend and I put another friend in an uncomfortable position.

How can I be so selfish?

But I can't control it!

How can I not control it? For crying out loud, I manage a church of eight hundred people! This is the dumbest thing. How stupid!

How can I let this get to me?

Then a bigger question.

What do I do tomorrow when I preach? What's going to happen?

I slumped into my chair, ate next to nothing, and fought back tears of shame.

One Of The Biggest Mistakes I Made

The biggest mistake I made when confronted with the idea of that fear was giving up opportunities to be around it. When I handed my friend that microphone, a part of me died, and fear did a victory dance, then it put another mark on the scorecard.

I can only tell you that I know you've given up something important to you. I know you've given up on opportunities, given up on relationships, and given up on something good that God planned for you.

I'm really sorry to hear that. And on the authority of God's word, I tell you that it isn't what God intends for you. I think at some point we have to say enough is enough. We can only offer fear so much space in our lives before we do a realistic assessment and think of another way.

A better way.

Freddy Kreuger Versus Pennywise The Clown

The first movie I recollect seeing in my life was *A Nightmare on Elm Street*. I was very young (maybe second or third grade). I remember specifically my dad and my sister telling me to cover my eyes during the "bad parts."

I didn't cover nothin'!

To be fair, I was mature at my age.

This is the part where the Christians reading this start to blog about how horrible I am, or how the pages of this book have been kissed by the devil's midwife.

Let's just pretend that maybe you saw *Night-*

mare on Elm Street. And maybe you and I have an understanding. And maybe we won't admit it to anyone.

In the pivotal and almost final scene, the protagonist Nancy is standing in a bedroom alone with Freddy Krueger—the quick-witted embodiment of evil.

There is a crucial part of dialogue. She defies him and says, "I know the secret now, this is just a dream, you're not alive."

As she turns around, he tries to attack her one final time, but is vaporized by her apathy.

The moral: if you turn your back and walk away, you're in the clear.

Let's look at another bad movie you probably shouldn't watch in grade school, Stephen King's *It*, recently remade and redone to terrify future generations with a sadistic murderous demonic clown. I wasn't as young when I saw *It* as I was when I saw Freddy, but I met Pennywise the clown when I was in grade school as well. I attribute my unique perspective and insight to early cultural exposure like this, but please don't do that to your kids.

It centers around a group of kids called the "Loser's Club." Together, they confront an ancient evil force that manifests itself as what you fear most, typically Pennywise the Clown. In case you haven't noticed, people either like the circus and clowns, or just mentioning clowns makes them want to relocate into the Clown Witness Protection Program (it's real, Google it. Just kidding, it's not.).

The story pivots around two major confrontations The Losers have with Pennywise the Dancing Demon Clown. The heroes of this story approach victory in an entirely different way than Nancy approached Freddy.

They believe the only way to stop *It* is to kill *it*.

Now, to fortify the science of all this, guess how many sequels *It* had. None. Freddy Krueger, on the other hand, had sequels, spinoffs, mini-series, side stories (I think he's in *Star Wars*), he hosts *The Tonight Show*, etc. He didn't die, and won't. Why? Because the protagonists keep turning their back on him. Every time they do that, he grows. They don't kill him. They're content with a momentary victory. The heroes of the story exchange a life free of terror for momentary avoidance.

One of the biggest mistakes I made when fighting anxiety took place during my friend's wedding. I sought an opportunity to abdicate the commitment I made to perform the reception benediction while simultaneously throwing one of his siblings in the awkward position of publicly speaking with no preparation.

Basically, I sucked.

I thought I could beat this by turning my back on it. I thought that even if I pretended that I was okay, and that this wasn't a big deal, it would disappear.

Couldn't. Have been. More. Wrong.

I learned that there are only two choices when fear grips your life. Frankly, it's not more complicated than that.

The first choice that most make is to turn their back on the fear and hope it disappears. If you think this is a viable option, put this book down. Seriously, go to the bookstore and see what their refund policy is. Rationalize with yourself that it's possible to live with fear and restricting yourself from certain aspects of life is better than dealing with it head on.

Turn your back on it.

However, there is a second option. And that's the option we'll exclusively explore for our remaining time together.

If you believe that you were never meant to live life this way, under terror's tyranny, then you're ready to make your move. If you believe that anxiety isn't a pet you're supposed to house train, that three nights out of five it pees on your new carpet (yeah you get a new carpet every five days, just follow me), then keep reading. If you believe time is precious, and you've given enough of it over to anxiety, then let's get together and figure out how to kill this freaking thing.

It's gonna be messy, and I'd be foolish to think that all the answers are through my knowledge and experience. But if I can get you to feel a little better, just a little more relaxed and less imprisoned, and if

I can make you laugh in the process, then my job will be done.

Choice 2: Run Toward Fear, And KILL IT

Let's get to it

If you are the type of person used to accommodating fear, then you most likely would have never picked this book up. That's why I'm certain you're interested in another way, but this way defies what appears conventional.

You can run toward fear, and KILL IT.

Yes, that's what I said. Run toward it. Kill it.

No, I don't be smokin' nothin'. I mean that the only way that you truly become a fear assassin is to kill it like you're a trained fear ninja.

How does this work?

Well, let's look at the Goliath story and see how this played out.

> "When the Philistine arose and came and drew near to meet David, David *ran quickly toward* the battle line to meet the Philistine."
>
> — 1 SAMUEL 17:48, ESV, EMPHASIS MINE

Yes, that's right. He ran QUICKLY TOWARD THE BATTLE LINE.

That's not a typo. There wasn't a Hebrew scribe that was having a bad day and decided to get even with his boss by telling a completely asinine story that didn't happen. While thousands of Israeli military stood at the sidelines, accommodating the embodiment of fear in their camps, this kid ran as quickly to face him as possible.

And to say that I messed up in this area is as much of an understatement as I could ever make.

Giving my friend the microphone to do the toast is staying at the camp. You not telling people how you are abused is staying at the camp. You not confronting your spouse about their money habits is staying at the camp.

Fear isn't going away. It's not getting any smaller.

And I found this out the hard way.

In the weeks following my initial panic attack, I became increasingly comfortable not speaking. I avoided it like you avoid those people in the middle of the mall that want to make all the fingers on your right hand shiny, but leave the left to look like a mangled stranger's hand.

Creatively, I started delegating. I started moving other people in position where I spoke less and less.

I'm grateful that I realized how detrimental this was early, because I was on a path to a pattern of fear accommodation.

When we accommodate fear, we live lives that were never meant to be ours. I was getting used to it.

And to tell you the truth, most days I fantasized about resigning. I stumbled at the idea of perhaps going to another church because I would have to give them my new list of pre-existing responsibilities that I was incapable of taking on as they hired me. I considered it like trying to get health insurance with a boat load of pre-existing conditions.

How would that interview look?

> **Interviewer:** Well, you definitely have the experience to do the job.
> **Pastor Sam:** Thanks, I'd love to work for your church.
> **Interviewer:** How do you feel about message preparation?
> **Pastor Sam:** I love message prep. It's my favorite thing. Honestly, that outfit looks dashing on you, really.
> **Interviewer:** Thanks, my wife picked it out. But seriously, how do you feel about speaking pretty regularly.
> **Pastor Sam:** Yeah, so here's the thing, I don't *speak* per se. I mean, I don't mind speaking to people as long as it's one-on-one and never in an arranged setting. Like I'm totally good just doing interviews like this.
> **I:** Wait, so you don't want to speak? Preach? How about leading meetings?
> **PS:** Well, I definitely can lead meetings, as

long as I don't have to attend the meetings I'm leading. I can do all the talking points over a video that I can edit, and you can just have someone there to facilitate. But as far as speaking in front of those people, maybe not.
I: This may pose a problem.
PS: But I am a good joke teller. I am a morale booster. I have decent hygiene like seventy percent of the time. I smell good. Why are you leaving? Why are you calling the police?

Yeah, that's how I envisioned it.

But as exaggerated as this story is, this is the end result of every person who has chosen to accommodate fear. We get used to the lingo of limitation, and we wear our anxiety like a banner.

And if you're reading this, there's no freaking way you are going to live like that anymore. No way.

Since we are talking about living a fear-free life and killing it, we probably should take a minute to discuss fear's origin.

The Origin Of Fear And Your Right To Kill It

Ever wonder where fear comes from? I don't mean neuroscience. I know about neurons firing and wiring and doing all kinds of bad to your mind.

But where does fear come from?

Whether you're a Christian or not, the Bible

gives some insight into this. You can take it or leave it. But for me, I had to take it.

> "...fear has to do with punishment, and whoever fears has not been perfected in love."
>
> — 1 John 4:18, ESV

According to this passage of Scripture, surface fear has to do with a deeper fear of what happens when we die—a primal fear of punishment and judgment awaiting in the afterlife.

The writer of *Amazing Grace*, John Newton, understood this well as he penned the following oft-quoted verse:

> *'Twas grace that taught my heart to fear*
> *And grace my fear relieved.*

As a pastor, it's my job to tell you that if you are concerned about the afterlife and you are fearful of slipping into a lost eternity, that fear is not misplaced.

This is not a theological treatment of Heaven or Hell, but the Bible describes only two destinations for those who have died. One leads to life everlasting. The other, not so much.

But the good news is the same verse that

discusses fear's origin discusses fear's ultimate defeat.

> *"There is no fear in love, but perfect love casts out fear.* For fear has to do with punishment, and whoever fears has not been perfected in love."
>
> — 1 JOHN 4:18, ESV, EMPHASIS MINE

Perfect love was given by Jesus when He gave His life for the sins of the world. We don't comprehend this, but Jesus suffered the punishment that contains fear's origin. Jesus died in our place. It's that simple. And then, He did the unthinkable by rising from the grave. Essentially, He took away the sting of death and offers us the true power of life through His Resurrection.

If you're not a Christian, this may seem foreign to you. And that's okay. My church is made up largely of people that never thought about Jesus before in this way.

If you are a Christian (having believed in what Jesus did for you) and you struggle with anxiety, you have to anchor yourself to this truth.

Moving from this, I'd like to ask you a question. I really want you to pay attention to how you answer.

Do you think that Jesus was born in a poor and infamous way, lived a life fraught with mockery and rejection, died a horrible humiliating death alone for your sins, rose again to conquer your sin and offer you eternity with Him (quick breath), and did this all just to call you into the bondage of crippling anxiety attacks, chronic fear, and severe depression?

When I originally stumbled onto that thought, I couldn't answer yes when I was in the midst of my planning. Of course, I believed that Jesus died to free me. Of course, I knew that I had nothing to fear after death. And yes, I didn't doubt God's ability to do the miraculous.

But to throw a corny preacher statement in here: the longest distance we have to travel is the twelve inches between our head and our heart.

I knew these things, but I wasn't subscribing to them. I was letting fear man the cockpit of my brain, and it was taking me places I never wanted to go.

Let's admit this quickly. Fear has already taken enough away from you. Why don't you run to that battle line armed with the perfect love of God and His truth? Let's quit accommodating fear—

—and kill it instead.

The Devil Is A Good Waiter

Half of my battle with anxiety brought me to the sobering reality time and time again that I think bears repeating.

The devil often has more patience than you.

He's good at waiting. We aren't. We want to consider something over, done, and broken. We want to label ourselves as crazy, without hope, or lost when it comes it comes to these battles. The devil doesn't jump so quickly.

Think about Jesus and his wilderness temptations. Three separate times Jesus was accosted by the devil and tempted. Each time, Jesus resists and it appears that the game is over. You never do *Rock, Paper, Scissors*, more than three times.

But Scripture doesn't say the devil gave up. Read the closing of that story.

> "And when the devil had ended every temptation, he departed from him until an opportune time."
>
> — Luke 4:13, ESV

An opportune time. That time for you might be a moment of weakness. That time might be a moment after a huge victory. That time might be when you're doing something mundane.

But the devil waits. He's a good waiter. If you had him in a restaurant, you would tip him well. See what I did right there?

Peter gives some more insight.

> "Be sober-minded; be watchful. Your

adversary the devil prowls around like a roaring lion, seeking someone to devour."

— 1 Peter 5:8, ESV

Seeking. He's not in a hurry. He's prowling. He's moving about, looking for something bad to get into.

So, what should we do? I'm going to suggest two things.

First, be patient. Don't give up so quickly. Don't assume defeat before you've even got into the thick of the battle with fear. And definitely, refuse to say that this will always be the way your life is. Sometimes, winning a battle is just outlasting your enemy.

Secondly, be aware that this is happening. This shouldn't scare you. If you are a believer, He that is in you is greater! You can't be scared, but you have to be aware. You have to be sober-minded. Your anxiety may come when you don't expect it. But you have to remember that sometimes healing is waiting and anticipating God to do something great.

The devil is patient because we aren't.

He is patient to attack while we are impatient with healing. Let's take a page from his playbook and just try to hold steady.

PART II
KNOW YOUR ENEMY

"When a resolute young fellow steps up to the great bully, the world, and takes him boldly by the beard, he is often surprised to find it comes off in his hand, and that it was only tied on to scare away the timid adventurers."

— Ralph Waldo Emerson

3

THE MONSTER IN THE SCIENCE LAB

I debated about putting a medical section in here, but that kinda goes against what I said previously about not being a medical professional. I interviewed two medical doctors about anxiety though, because I didn't want you to think that if you read this, you are committing to some opinion of a rather good-looking dynamic preacher that you have never had the pleasure to meet.

Because that's what you'd think, obvi.

Full disclosure: This is a married couple who are both doctors in different fields and happen to be two of my closest friends. Their names are Catherine and Scott.

Full disclosure (with irony): This is the couple whose wedding I was supposed to pray at and invariably ended up having a panic attack, abdicating my responsibility to the groom's brother. There's something funny about this.

I went through a couple questions with them that were rather pointed. I'm going to make it simple, consolidate their answers, and make it as easy to understand as I can.

How big of an issue is anxiety for most people?

It's big. Between five to eighteen percent of Americans claim to struggle with anxiety and panic attacks. That includes some that have a generalized panic disorder. We are talking millions of people here. What's most startling, Catherine said, is that only thirty-seven percent of those people seek any kind of treatment whether medical or psychological.

Thirty-seven percent.

What that says to me is that there are millions of people in private hells thinking they're all alone. They walk among us, feeling shame and feeling sick about who they are. And what the devil (yeah, I'm going there) has done has convinced them that they are alone.

What. A. Freaking. Scam.

Physiologically or neurologically, what causes a panic attack?

Scott said after having treated several people suffering through a panic attack, that the person really feels like they're going to die during a panic attack. They get the total package: shortness of breath, elevated heart rate like they just ran a marathon, sweat, dizziness, nausea, numbness in the extremities. It's pretty horrific.

But it's not deadly. In fact, it's triggered neurologically.

Catherine dove a little deeper on this. As it turns out, the panic is a completely normal physiological reaction brought about by the sympathetic nervous system.

To put it in plainer terms, we sense danger, perceived or otherwise. Our body responds by going into fight or flight. All of our being jumps in like a bunch of people with no rhythm jumping onto the dance floor at a wedding during the chicken dance (neither Catherine or Scott said this, I added it and you're welcome).

Essentially, your body is priming itself for danger. And it does a great job. Epinephrine and neural epinephrine go through your body, and you get the tingles, the shortness of breath, and the partridge in the pear tree. All of it, in response to the fear.

Now, let's go a little further with this. Typically, Catherine explained, people that suffer a panic attack become afraid of the symptoms. They actually become fearful of another panic attack, and a vicious circle begins. The panic attack becomes a natural response to thinking about a panic attack and it stays with you.

It's now happening regardless of the trigger.

And let's talk about the trigger. Panic is usually triggered by something that is actually going on in your life. Scott recounted of a patient who was having generalized anxiety and panic attacks and once the conversation was taken further, the gentlemen confessed that he was having problems at work and that he had been putting off having a difficult conversation. Thus, every time he thought of work—Panic City, baby.

Why do panic attacks tend to reoccur frequently after the initial one?

Because our brains suck (that's also mine). No, Catherine and Scott both offered insight. Typically, the situation that led to the attack doesn't easily get resolved (wayward children, money problems, sickness, fear of death) and panic signs the lease in your life. If these life occurrences are resolved, panic tends to find another place to lodge. But sometimes, the cycle of panic needs to be broken.

Frankly, that's the whole point of this book.

But again, we no longer fear the situation, we start to fear the fear of the situation. Panic becomes the center focus and you see it everywhere, like an obsessed girlfriend that shows up at all of your sporting events until you finally have to talk to her. I just married mine. Well, I never played sports, and I was a little obsessed with her first, but you get the gist.

What types of medication are typically prescribed and what are the most common side effects from the medications given to help people with anxiety?

Personal note, and please hear me on this. I am not against medication for anxiety or depression. Not at all. In fact, on more than one occasion, I inquired about taking medication for my panic attacks. Here's the cold truth about why I didn't: I read online that the side effect of a lot of the commonly-prescribed medications produced—get this—more panic attacks. And considering I was speaking publicly just about every other week during these attacks, I couldn't get it loaded in my system with enough time to experience the benefits of the relief. That's honestly why. Trust me, if you would have told me to take elephant tranquilizer I would have just negotiated where the shot was going to go.

But typically, these medications prescribed are anti-depressants and anti-anxiety (shocker) medications. They have some pretty gnarly side effects, though. I'm not going to go into all of them, but to paraphrase Catherine, you definitely incur some disruption of your life.

If you're struggling with debilitating fear, though, what's the alternative?

I'm so glad you asked. Because so did I.

In your opinion, what's the best alternative to mediation?

Catherine said there are some behaviors that really reduce that panic. First, exercise. I'm going to jump on this train. One physical thing that I added to my routine for defeating fear is running thirty minutes at least every day on the elliptical. I mean, I exercised on that thing like a madman. It really helped me to get more control of the panic. I would feel the general foreboding coming on and I would run faster. I would imagine the fear being worn out by being in my body and give up for the day so I could preach that night or the next morning.

Now, that's not exactly a medical thought, and I know some of you imagined fear punching a time clock and saying "Peace, Out," but believe it or not, it has some medical validity. Exercise does help to reduce anxiety.

Also, you can reduce caffeine (it's not a silver bullet, I tried it, but it didn't hurt), eat healthy (I didn't do that, there's a Burger King next to my gym), and give up smoking and alcohol as well.

But those are just little things to help. Both Scott and Catherine talked at length about something that is more pertinent to you finishing the rest of this book. Something both of them referred to as CBT.

Cognitive Behavioral Therapy.

This, I did do. This, anyone can do. And frankly, this book, in a very elementary way, is an offshoot of CBT.

Essentially, CBT is a solution-focused therapy plan where a person works on the thought patterns causing the present undesired state. That's a fluffy way to say that it's a method to help you fix your broken thoughts. There's science behind it, and a whole lot of success. In fact, both Catherine and Scott agreed that the results of CBT and the results of taking psychotropic medication have similar outcomes with regards to anxiety and panic attacks.

I didn't really know what CBT was until I went to a therapist myself. Again, I don't think any one thing is a silver bullet to eliminate panic. But if you get enough bullets firing at the same time, and you keep at it, BOOM (but that's what we are here to talk about, isn't it?).

What would you say to someone right now that's struggling with clinical anxiety disorder or frequent panic attacks?

At the onset, both Catherine and Scott mentioned that if you are having a panic attack and you're worried that it's a heart attack, you should seek treatment from a physician. I agree too, mainly because I don't want you to sue us if you have a heart attack and say, "Sam said to just assume panic and kill your fear and now I'm dead."

Guess you wouldn't be talking if you're dead, but just follow me.

Of course, if you're not sure what it is, seek treatment. But, if they say anxiety, then let's do business, shall we?

What both Catherine and Scott emphasized was that you should do something. If you are where I was and panic attacks have become your permanent plus one, then you shouldn't allow that to be your new normal. Catherine emphasized that you're not alone. Millions of people are struggling with anxiety and they remain silent about it. Scott said you can recover. You can get over it. You can win.

And I promise you this, you are not alone. When I shared with my church about my struggle to overcome fear, the number of people that reached out to me to thank me and also to confess their own solitary struggle was overwhelming. It was both encouraging and also challenging to think of all these suffering people. And you are one of them. You can win.

But you have to make the choice. Sound familiar?

If you're still reading, let's step it up, and really get into some of the tactics that fear uses against you. But first, we are going to start with fear's most trusted ally and accomplice, and the one who does the greatest amount of work to make sure fear stays put in our lives.

I'm talking, of course, about ourselves.

4

FIND THE "ME" IN ENEMY

I sat in the counselor's chair waiting for the session to continue. It was a larger room, not like an office but more like a living room, with a couple couches, a couple love seats and some chairs. If you've ever been to a counselor (I'd highly recommend it if you haven't), they often have more than one option for you to sit. I think this is a part of the evaluation process.

Oh, check him out. He picked the executive chair that I usually sit in. Yeah, that shows me he is a narcissist and wants to dominate the people around him.

Oh yeah, of course, he picks the most uncomfortable seat. He wants to punish himself because he thinks he deserves it.

Yeah, I've thought all this stuff through.

While the counselor and I spoke over weeks, we dealt with panic. But one of the most valuable lessons I learned was the ability to dig a little a deeper to see what the underlying issue was.

Because, it wasn't just related to a nineteen step walk to the pulpit. And there's a great chance that the panic you feel and the general anxiety that has been torturing you has a deeper message for you.

And as we will discuss more, fear lies, a lot.

I am going to get real here. This is going to be the hardest thing that I write in this book. I've been transparent about my journey thus far, but I hesitate sharing this.

Remember the words that came into mind when I was late for the platform that night. *I'm not ready. I can't do this. I'm not ready.*

I chose to focus on those thoughts. So what if I wasn't ready to get to the platform? Who cares? I'd be ready in ten seconds!

So, we dug.

At the time of my panic attack, my wife was pregnant with our first child. We waited close to ten years before we had our first. And the feeling of being a dad is beyond any great thing I can say. But as it turned out, I had a greater worry overtaking my thoughts. The simple thought that I wasn't ready to be a dad. I wasn't ready to be a man that provides for someone so dependent. I felt that I would fail. I felt like I'd be every dad of every sitcom ever, dumb, helpless, and just there to make jokes (some of that is kinda true).

But really, I felt I would hurt my daughter.

So I followed that thought with the counselor. I followed it to expose the lie. The same lie you have. The lie that plagues so many.

I wasn't enough. I wasn't good enough. I wasn't going to be able to do what was required of me. Translated out as, "I'm not ready."

I found myself so overwhelmed with emotions. I felt a dam open up in my heart and out poured this poison and infection. I visualized myself holding her in the hospital and holding back because I wasn't ready. I pictured myself bringing her home, thinking that she should be anyone's but mine. Because I wasn't ready. I wasn't good enough. I wasn't the right fit.

This faithless lie had embedded itself like a parasite into my thought patterns. I felt like that dude in *Alien* (the one from the seventies) when he woke up from the coma and was hungry but felt a little off. That's because there was a wicked monster about rip through his body and become a murderer.

Now, that's kind of a joke, but not really. If you are subscribed to a lie, a repeated thought, something that is causing you to have constant panic, you most certainly are going to be dominated by fear. Fear plays a crooked game. Anxiety makes you believe stuff that you'd never say out loud.

I became woefully aware that God was not honored by this lie, and it was impeding my ability to enjoy this stage of my life. No, I didn't entertain it any longer. No, I didn't need someone to tell me I was good enough.

I recognized the lie, and removed it. Sure, I'm not going to be a perfect dad. But an imperfect dad that shows up in courage is better than perfect one that flees in fear. I am who I am. And I'm gonna mess this kid up just like you messed your kids up and how you were messed up.

But I will love her with every ounce of my being and my care. And God's grace will be there to fill in the cracks left by my sin.

That's the thought I replaced it with. I was liberated. It hurt, but I was post op now. Uphill climb: complete. Now, it was time to take what I knew and apply it to the pattern of fear.

I was really angry that Jamie made me go to the counselor, and even more angry when I came home from that session with the remnants of ugly cry face still on my mug. You know what I'm talking about. There's the tearful glance Hollywood style and then there is the face that has actually transformed into someone else's face because the tears have permanently changed it.

That's what happened in the counselor's office. But I had to dig, extract, and replace. And you need to do the same.

Let's stop for a minute. I'm not a Cognitive Behavioral Therapist, but what deep thought is permeating your fear? What agony is that fear concealing? Are you worried you're not good enough? Worried that you are less than? Are you worried that you don't have the strength?

Getting to the root of those nasty thoughts tips the scales in your favor and sends anxiety packing.

But don't get excited yet. Knowledge, in this case, is only a piece of the puzzle. We still have work to do, and knowing that a lie is at the root helps you to be more confident about walking in truth.

Remember, we are still talking about what we are doing that causes anxiety to treat our lives like a permanent Airbnb So, what else do we do?

Philippians 8:4 (Opposite Day)

You don't have to be a Christian in order to appreciate when you're doing something opposite of what the Bible says. Sometimes people do it purposefully in defiance. Other times, we do it out of pure ignorance.

We are going to head into that lane right now. There's something that we, who struggle with anxiety, do that is completely opposite of what the Bible teaches. And fear loves it when you do this.

Here's the premise:

There is an oft-quoted passage of Scripture in the New Testament from Paul.

> "Rejoice in the Lord always; again I will say, rejoice. Let your reasonableness be known to everyone. The Lord is at hand; do not be anxious about anything, but in everything by prayer and supplication with thanksgiving let your requests be made known to God. And the peace of God, which surpasses all understanding, will guard your hearts and your minds in Christ Jesus. Finally, brothers, whatever is true, whatever is honorable, whatever is just, whatever is pure, whatever is lovely, whatever is commendable, if there is any excellence, if there is anything worthy of praise, think about these things."
>
> — PHILIPPIANS 4:4–8, ESV

This is the Scripture. It's dealing with mindset. Very fitting considering the Apostle Paul penned this from a jail cell. Mindset was the only thing he could control.

Anxiety imprisons you. And as we talked about, you can't control the thoughts that enter your mind, but you absolutely can control the thoughts that you focus on. It's one thing to see a train wreck, it's another to stop your car, grab popcorn and stare at carnage.

Unfortunately, we tend to do the opposite of what Paul instructed.

"...in everything by prayer and supplication with thanksgiving..." Are you grateful? Fear strips you of your gratitude. Show me someone paralyzed with fear and I will show you someone who is incapable of gratitude because the joy of their heart has been dammed up by thoughts of dread. Gratitude is a key to overcoming the pain of fear.

"...let your requests be made known unto God..." Do you pray? Have you taken this burden to God in prayer or are you relying on your own mental fortitude to carry the victory of the day? Praying is unloading. Praying is focusing. And if we pray, our minds are fixed on a conversation with God that is liberating, instead of the common conversation we have with ourselves that is suffocating.

"...whatever is true...think on these things..." Is what you're fearful of true? Of course, this is where you'll say *it has POTENTIAL* to be true. Sure, it does. But that's not what this verse says. This verse says to focus on what is true. Remember, rooted in your fear is some lie.

"...Whatever is honorable...think on these things..." Is this thought giving honor? Does it add to your faith? Does it add to the quality of your conversation? If not, focus should be diverted from it.

"...Whatever is just, pure, lovely, commend-

able..." Do you see the pattern? If these words threw a party, would your thoughts be invited? Or would they be awkwardly snubbed because they come early and leave late, eating the party-thrower out of house and home?

Here's the deal, I'll say it again.

You can't control what comes into your mind, but you can control how long it stays and how comfortable it is staying there. If you can learn to control what you can control when it comes to your thinking, submit it to God, and allow your thoughts to be ruthlessly filtered through this lens, anxiety will not be comfortable staying in the center of your mind.

But this takes work.

Your mind is wired to think a certain way after a while. The good news is that you're the general contractor of your mind. You can rewire it at any time. We do this so often that we don't realize. You are constantly adapting, changing, and accommodating situations because of how strong your mind is.

The product: Peace. Paul talks about the peace that passes all understanding. It's a direct result that comes from this ninja-like control of your mind. It's the target of this. You can calm the mental storm. Remember, you can pray that God takes it away, but unless you're willing to change what you're doing, he may not honor that half-heartedness.

We are going to devote a ton more time on how

to control our thoughts, but right now, know that you are probably letting fear drive the thought bus.

Let's look at another way that we help anxiety do its work.

Allow Yourself To Feel Good

There are things that no one tells you when you talk to them about chronic anxiety. I want to tell you something that you need to know.

You can still enjoy things. Yes. When you have a victory, you can enjoy the victory. When you have a win, you can celebrate with a big piece of cake (well, that's what I want to do; maybe you prefer kale, in which case you don't like joy and should seriously not be reading this part).

Throughout the time I spent fighting with anxiety, I had such difficulty taking a commercial break from it. It was always on my mind, like the Willie Nelson song (Elvis sang it first).

When I went to dinner, I found myself catatonically looking off to the side reminiscing about the panic attack I had earlier like it was some overseas love that had just sent me a letter. I caught myself daydreaming of dread when I was playing with my daughter. I found myself having thoughts about pain in the night when I was watching a movie with my wife.

Truth, when I preached that first sermon in

January I felt victorious—like Joel Osteen's dentist. I got up and I made it through. I should have celebrated that as a win. But instead, fear forced me to move past the victory and be wrapped up in "what if" thoughts. I couldn't celebrate, even though I had a lot to be grateful for.

We have to take good times in the midst of the bad. We can't allow fear to rob us of good things that have nothing to do with being fearful. This was something that happened to me over time, and it crept up into every area of my life. I just let the trespassing happen, like an absentee homeowner comfortable letting squatters use my bathroom sink to clip their toenails. (Yuck, what a terrible visual illustration).

Our lives always being bad is an illusion fear creates to keep you from getting some wins on the scoreboard. It's a farce. And we need to feel good when it's good. We also need to celebrate when we are able to overcome, even if it's just powering through a panic attack. If we don't get traction with victory, we'll forget what it's like to experience enjoyment. We'll forget what it's like to think of anything except for fear.

There's more going on in your life than that!

Your Bucket Is Empty

"What do you do for fun," the counselor asked me.

"I...umm...I," cue crickets.

I couldn't answer the question because I'm not a very "fun" person. I'm not a person who does things for fun. I work a lot. And that time, I worried a lot. But what the counselor said next gave me the license to pursue fun a little more.

"Your bucket is empty," she said as she looked at me knowingly.

It was cool because up until a minute ago, I wasn't even aware that there was a bucket. Also, I was unaware that it was empty. Further, I didn't know I was in charge of filling said imaginary, newly-arrived bucket.

But she was right.

I had quit putting in good. I had allowed everything to be business.

Business wasn't booming. It was looming. And I was crippled by panic. So, I wrote myself a list of things in my schedule that I needed to do. Your list may look different.

Here goes:

Go to the bookstore. As long as I can remember, I had a beautiful connection to the bookstore. The smells, books on shelves even lighting, coffee, dreams. Yes, dreams. If you've ever wondered what dreams smell like—it's the bookstore.

But I always dreamed in the bookstore. I dreamed of being a person of influence whose words would one day be read by another. There were names on those pages whose lives were immortalized by print. And their ideas change people.

The bookstore is my utopia. I can never go quickly. I have to stay long. And every time I go, it's never enough. I read wide. I read everything. I love reading. I love writing.

And I had done none of this while in panic mode. I quit doing it. So, I took my anxiety-laden soul to a Barnes & Noble. Opening the door, I expected nothing to happen.

But I was wrong. I felt like someone had plugged me into a wall outlet and energy was pulsing into my lifeless carcass. I looked around the books, and dared to dream again. I ordered a coffee and thumbed through fiction. I let myself leave the panic at the door and I retreated into a familiar place of comfort. Fear couldn't touch it.

This is where you stop reading and think of something that has nothing to do with anxiety.

Dream about an anxiety-free life.

"It's not real," you say.

Well, let me gently remind you that neither is your fear that keeps plaguing you. Right now, it's hypothetical.

So what if I wasn't on the bestseller list next to Stephen King? I was becoming a child again. A fearless one. I was careless in that store. I was careless because nothing could touch me there. I tapped into the part of my mind that allowed me to be happy. And fear starts to get nervous when you get joy.

Get Moving

When people know that you have panic attacks, they begin telling you all the ways they've heard you can get rid of them.

"Try breathing into a bag!"

Nope, didn't work for me.

"Give up caffeine."

Yeah, tried that. Didn't have a coffee for six months. Not only was I panicked, but tired all the time. Beautiful.

"Exercise!"

Now that one, that's a little different. There aren't many things in this book that I've given you to do apart from mental exercise and spiritual discipline, but here's my experience with exercise:

Before panic attacks, I was working out pretty regularly. However, it wouldn't take heaven and earth moving to get me to miss. Wish I could tell you it did.

But I began to do something Jon Acuff wrote about with regard to having a panic attack. He said, "Exercise like your life depends on it."

For me, that meant hitting the elliptical. I don't

run outside because I live in Pittsburgh, so on most days, it's raining, and on the other days, it's colder than a mother-in-law's shoulder. And I'm not one of those people that you see running in snow and rain because I don't hate myself. Sorry, you disciplined lads and lasses, that's just not my jam.

So, I started going to the gym every single day. I would wake up and run on the elliptical. Because of my panicked state, I would often have thoughts of anxiety, and it would cause a mini panic attack right there on the machine. The fact that I was running helped me to power through it.

Extraordinarily, when I would get off the machine, even if it was just for a little bit, I felt better. And the day was a little more manageable.

Now, even though I'm not a doctor, anyone can Google the effects that exercise has on your mental health. Dopamine and endorphins are released into your brain. I pictured every time I completed a workout, those little soldiers marching around my brain with M16's shooting at anxiety's fortified strongholds.

It really helped.

Plus, from a purely mental standpoint, when I would feel like I got winded going up the steps before preaching, and feel as though I couldn't breathe, I would say out loud to myself, "You just ran twenty-four miles this week, you can handle a walk up fourteen steps. This is in your mind."

I have to say it helped. And it made me feel healthier. And it helped with weight control, which for me is a huge bonus.

If you don't exercise at all, and you would say, "I could never go to a gym, or run on a machine, or anything like that." That's fine. But what is it that you can do?

Would a walk around the neighborhood be feasible? Would you be able to do a Jillian Michaels exercise video? Would you be able to do some push-ups, sit-ups, jump rope? How about swimming?

These are all on the table. I'm not saying this will rid you of anxiety, but I'm saying don't refuse help. Don't refuse something that could make you feel even ten percent better.

Run towards fear, both spiritually and physically.

5

SPIRITUAL WARFARE BOOTCAMP

How long have you been in this battle? How long have you been fighting anxiety? How much have you prayed that it would go away?

I know that for some of us, it's been a long time. And part of our faith is tested because we feel that something is misfiring. We feel that God is either unwilling or incapable of answering us.

Please don't take what I'm saying as blasphemous, but our minds go there. It's natural because we asked, and God said no.

I want to look quickly at an old Bible story, one of the most famous ones in fact. It took place in a time of great trial for the nation of Israel. A young Hebrew man named Daniel was taken into captivity by the enemies of God. The king demanded that prayer cease throughout the land, and if not, there would be punishment.

So, Daniel decided to open up his window and pray like a contestant on *The Voice*. Come on, I wanna be on team Adam! Turn your chair at my prayer!

Daniel didn't seem to care what the outcome was. So, he was arrested and then ordered to be executed.

When we think of execution, we think lethal injection, or a little worse, the electric chair. Even more primitive: hanging.

Not so fast.

Daniel was ordered to be thrown into a den of flipping lions! Lions! Like roaring, muscular, people-make-motivational-posters-with-pictures-of-them LIONS.

They throw him in this pit with lions, and then they take the night off.

The scene the following morning is earth-shattering.

> "Then, at break of day, the king arose and went in haste to the den of lions. As he came near to the den where Daniel was, he cried out in a tone of anguish. The king declared to Daniel, "O Daniel, servant of the living God, has your God, whom you serve continually, been able to deliver you from the lions?" Then Daniel said to the king, "O king, live forever! My

> God sent his angel and s*hut the lions' mouths*, and they have not harmed me, because I was found blameless before him; and also before you, O king, I have done no harm.""
>
> — DANIEL 6:19–22, ESV, EMPHASIS MINE

Now, in Sunday school, this teaches really well! But here's something you might have missed.

Dude was in a lions' den, all night, with a lid on. All night long, Lionel Richie.

Also, another part you might be missing is the part where it says, "...My God sent his angel and shut the lions' mouths..."

Did you catch that? What do you think went on in that den? When I was younger in my faith, I always envisioned Daniel cuddling with the lions and reading them Bible stories, and maybe they'd eat some of Daniel's snack packs that he brought. God didn't put them in another room, didn't start a lion Netflix where the lions would binge-watch Lion *Stranger Things*. That's not what happened at all. The lions didn't eat Daniel for lack of trying! He said an angel came down and shut their mouths!

That means they charged at him! That means Daniel saw them try to open their mouths. That means this is the scariest freaking thing ever! Are you kidding? Like God didn't put him in a bubble of glass? God didn't make the lions talk and tell him it was all good like he made Balaam's Donkey talk in Numbers? No. These lions were mad and hungry. They were hangry!

Just because you have faith, doesn't mean the journey will be fear-free. This isn't what you wanted. This isn't what you imagined battling, but if God allows you to survive it, you're ahead. If God has given you this day, it's a good thing!

Don't expect your faith to ensure the victory takes place overnight. My battle with anxiety was nine months. That's 270 days. That's a lot of sleeps and wake-ups. That's a lot of middle of the night pain. But you can't allow what you know to be true of God to be diminished by the length of your battle.

If Daniel had to hang out with lions, anxiety is gonna knock more than once. But just like Daniel, deliverance is on the way. It might not be the way you wanted, but it's coming.

Jesus Stayed And Prayed

If there was one question that lingers in the mind of most Christians and that pastors don't deal with quite well, it is this:

Why does God allow_____?

That blank has numerous objects placed on it from time to time.

Suffering.

Evil.

Loss.

Death.

And in our case, anxiety. Panic.

We don't deal well with this question for two reasons. We have to force our minds into one of two camps typically.

First camp: God knows intimately how this will hurt us but carelessly permits it to happen anyway. Sure, you've heard that person. *Well, how could God allow those children to suffer, he must not care.* Or, *God must not love me, or my wife would still be here. He had to have known how painful this is.*

Those conversations will always cycle back to the central idea that God knows, permits, and sometimes causes but doesn't care. It's a damaging proposition for sure.

Second camp: God knows intimately about how this will hurt us, but he can't do anything about it. This comes down to *Where was God when this tragedy happened? Wasn't God powerful enough to stop it? Why would I pray when God is incapable of preventing this?*

This idea proposes that God has weakness when it comes to the brokenness that we experience. It denies his ability, more than his willingness. Comparable to a parent that sees his child going down a bad road and he stands watching and crying as the child meets bad consequences and perhaps even demise.

Both are faulty because they deny three common things that we know of God and life.

The first is that of purpose. Perhaps it isn't that God allowed us to experience horrible things ruthlessly, but lovingly. His love enables us to find purpose even in pain. Dare I say, purpose even in panic? Yeah, that means that there is something here that's valuable. A valuable lesson, valuable growth and more valuable time spent seeking God's face and not just His hand when a situation overwhelms us.

I believe that when we reach eternity, we will regard the times we spent seeking God with reckless abandon to be the most unbelievably rewarding times of our lives, though that seeking took place in pockets of desperation.

The second thing we ignore is identification. We forget how much Jesus suffered. Jesus is our example and we see that God the Father doesn't spare Him an ultimate excruciating (literally) experience to bring about a beautiful purpose.

We are tempted to say, well, that was Jesus, he was God in the flesh. God can handle it. It didn't mean anything to him. If you think that, you simply haven't spent any time in the garden of Gethsemane.

> "And he withdrew from them about a stone's throw, and knelt down and prayed, saying, "Father, if you are

willing, remove this cup from me. Nevertheless, not my will, but yours, be done." And there appeared to him an angel from heaven, strengthening him. And being in agony he prayed more earnestly; and his sweat became like great drops of blood falling down to the ground."

— Luke 22:41–44, ESV

Do you see anything exciting here where Jesus is saying, "Wow, this is gonna be so simple"?

No. We see agony, sweat, anticipation, and even a plea to heaven for the brutality of the cross to pass from him.

But heaven remains closed because God's purposes remain perfect.

Luke even recounts that an angel came and strengthened him. An angel. But he still was in agony. And he sweat drops of blood.

There's a medical account that says this is a rare condition known as hematidrosis. A condition where the body is in such a state of unrest that blood secretes from the pores of the skin.

So, do you still think that Jesus had no feeling for this?

But that's not what we're missing here. We are missing identification.

Jesus the God-man endured hardship. If we want to follow him, we will identify with struggle. Always.

Finally, we overlook the curse. This world is cursed. It's fallen. It's broken. It's as damaged as we are. I can spend pages and pages examining the hows and whys, but I believe that this curse was invited by Adam, and visited on us. I believe that this is a curse that we will bear regardless of how holy we become. This world is troublesome, and we are in exile here. If we expect that life will be hard, you will feel blessed when it's easy or hard. If we expect that life will be full of utopia-like blessing, we will have difficulty finding joy in either.

Knowing that the world is cursed is enough to understand that we are in for some serious crap. But we must take refuge in the God that plans purpose and also identifies with the troubles we experience. Jesus is clear about this world.

> "I have said these things to you, that in me you may have peace. In the world you will have tribulation. But take heart; I have overcome the world."
>
> — John 16:33, ESV

We take heart not in the fact that this world will be free of fear, but that Jesus has overcome it.

This is all a long-winded way for me to say that

God has planned purpose in your battle with fear. There is something that you need to understand about that pain. There is something that you need to do as a result. If you play your cards right and react in faith instead of recoil in bitterness, you will be joyous that you've come through the battle.

When Jesus went to Heaven, the Bible says that he was glorified as He sat at the right hand of the father. All the purpose that God weaves into our battles will be realized when we see Him. It will all be worth it. All of it. I promise.

6

TOOLS OF THE TORTURER

The man stabbed me in the heart with a dagger.

I like opening a sentence this way so you say, "How is he writing with a dagger in his heart?"

To which I would refer you to the movie *Iron Man*. Anything is possible with money and technology!

Unfortunately, I haven't an abundance of either. And he theoretically didn't stab me with an actual dagger.

Well, he didn't stab me at all.

No, he did something else.

He tried to encourage me.

So, here's the story. I was three months into my journey with panic attacks. Every time I would get up to the platform, I would have a horrible anxiety attack right before getting to the platform. I would get through it, by the skin of my teeth, do what I had to do, and get back off the platform feeling absolutely and utterly defeated (like I was getting over the flu).

At the four-month marker, I was shaking hands at the door after the last of four services I preached that weekend, and a man looked at me and shook my hand with a huge toothy Tom-Cruise-on-the-Oprah- show kinda smile.

"Man," he said. "You must be so blessed."

"I am," I answered emphatically. Because if you're in a church and someone uses the word blessed and you don't agree with them, there is no way you're a Christian. That is grounds for removal from the pew.

"No seriously, you must be so blessed. To be able to do this, with such joy, and bring so much joy to others through the Bible. I've only been coming here four weeks, but I just am so encouraged leaving here week after week. Thank you for what you do." He exits stage right.

Now, any other pastor would be reeling at this amazing bit of verbal scrumptiousness. For a people-pleaser, this would have put you in euphoria.

But it took every bit of my remaining strength not to begin to cry right there in the midst of the church.

You see, I was about 100,000 miles south of encouraged.

I had developed a predictable pattern. I would fight panic attacks every weekend, I would get up to do announcements or preach, then I would come home, and I would lie in bed in my church clothes as though I just ran twenty-six miles in 100-degree heat having just eaten a McDonald's breakfast (come on, you know what McDonald's breakfast does if you try to do physical things after eating). I sometimes would cry for a moment; other times I would simply look at the ceiling and reminisce about a day that I used to do this without being paralyzed by fear.

Heart-stopping, encouragement-stripping, anointing-sapping fear.

This had become my normal.

And I have a feeling you sympathize.

And most of you, you probably empathize.

You're Doing The Right Things

There is a good number of us that do the wrong things when anxiety strikes us at our core.

I wasn't in that place. I didn't go off into moral failing. I didn't get a side-chick. I didn't go gamble. I didn't watch porn. In fact, I prayed more in 2016 than I had my entire life. I read more Scripture and ripped through the Bible, desperately searching and reaching for God like a man looking for his ID at the TSA check in an airport.

I'm going to state this at the onset: You may be doing the right things.

You may be in counseling. You may be treating those around you with kindness and compassion. You may even be hiding your anxiety and bearing the burden selflessly on your own.

And I promise you, those are all good things.

But may I tell you what I never did?

I never examined Fear's Greatest Hits. Meaning, I never really looked for patterns in what was happening, even though I had developed a pretty amazing routine with fear at the center of my life.

I especially didn't examine the Scriptural references that describe such patterns with regards to fear.

Essentially, I had the opportunity to study the enemy's (fear's) toolbox, and found I hadn't taken it.

Well that changed one day. And that day was the day that I discovered fear's toolbox. If you can crack the code of fear, you can kill it.

So, let's give it a go.

Tool #1: Fear Sets Unreasonable Terms

I said that most of my insight about fear came from the Goliath story. Specifically, Goliath himself. He was the evil leader of the Philistine army that wanted to pulverize God's people.

I know. Kinda dark, right.

But in really examining Goliath, I caught a glimpse of fear's hand. And it was worth the glance. I could go read a hundred books about David, God's chosen man and anointed would-be king. But if I wanted to see what fear was doing to me, I needed to become a biographer of Goliath.

So, let's have a look.

> "He stood and shouted to the ranks of Israel… *Choose a man for yourselves*, and let him come down to me."
>
> — 1 Samuel 17:8, ESV, emphasis mine

Here is a single soldier who is challenging an entire army. But what he was actually doing was custom at the time. Malcolm Gladwell has amazing insight about this from his book, *David and Goliath* (how do you like that?). Gladwell explains that Goliath was attempting to engage in something known as "single combat." This was something very common in this culture. Two opposing sides sought to avoid heavier bloodshed of an actual battle by each choosing a warrior for a duel.

Goliath goes into the valley called Elah. Some Bible teachers refer to this as the Valley of Fear (Come on, now!). And he commands Israel to send another challenger to match him.

There are two big issues with this.

First, in order for Israel to send someone down there, this person would need to sacrifice the high ground. Both armies are on equal level with a valley in between. And I don't know if you have ever read about the Philistines, but honor wasn't high on their list of priorities.

There's a second problem with this situation.

Last I checked, unless I'm missing something in the narrative, Israel didn't have a giant to combat the Philistine's giant. I think he called in sick that month or your mother-in-law was unavailable.

Are my mother-in-law jokes too much?

One time my mother-in-law confronted me for making too many jokes about her from the platform when I was preaching. My response: "Did you think those were jokes?"

Anyhoo, maybe Israel's warrior was taking some R & R and playing some basketball, exhausted from doing other giant stuff, like always getting the canned goods from the top shelf and so on and so forth. Either way, he was MIA. They didn't have a person that could go toe-to-toe with Goliath, and a victory for the Philistines was all but guaranteed.

Either way, Goliath set the terms. And Israel was playing by those terms.

Allow me to introduce you to the first tool in fear's toolbox.

Fear Sets Unreasonable Terms

It was positively unreasonable for Israel to enter

a victory-by-combat situation with this Philistine monster.

Just as unreasonable as it was for them, it's unreasonable for you.

What have you accepted as your reality? Specifically, what battle does fear tell you to enter that God may not want you to fight? What rules has fear set for you?

Mine was pretty specific.

Fear said, "You have to speak with total confidence without having a panic attack or else you shouldn't be doing this. You lose. You're a fraud. You're unfaithful. If you show the church you're afraid, you'll hurt the church, yourself, and the future of the church's leadership."

Why was this rule was so unsettling? Well, at the time of this writing my role is the associate pastor, but it's the church's plan to install me as the senior pastor to succeed the founding pastor. I've been in this role since 2004. I've invested a lot into it. It's a part of me and it's a part of my future.

But fear counted me as disqualified. And to be honest, I played by fear's terms. I imagined resigning and going somewhere else where I didn't have to speak.

Fear setting the terms like this all but destroyed me. I constantly felt like garbage every time I would speak. Even when I wasn't speaking, this thought would invade my mind.

Somehow, I associated spiritual victory and leadership boldness with a lack of uncertainty and complete confidence.

That was my victory by single combat. So, I constantly labeled myself a terrible leader.

How about you? Where are you letting fear set the terms? Do you have anxiety at your job if you don't perform slightly higher than you did last quarter? Does that make you sick to your stomach if you lose that client?

Do you feel if you have a night where your kids need to be corrected that you're failing as a parent and your kids aren't blessed to have you as a parent?

What about new moms? Honestly, I am so grateful that I grew up being raised by a woman without social media, because fear is setting some whacky and unreasonable terms for mothers. Consequently, you have moms (and dads) that have no parenting voice of their own, and are trying to keep up with the social media Joneses (who are most likely lying).

Fear is setting unreasonable terms.

Do you equate a lack of conflict in your home with effective parenting? Good, keep that up and your kids will be driving your car when they're three.

I can take you to a thousand homes where there is hardly a raised voice anywhere, but the kids are dying for structure and discipline.

Do you feel that because you aren't doing something your parent wants you to do you are failing? Perhaps you are positioned to take over the family business, but you have ideas of your own on how it should go. Fear says you have to do it the way you've always done it. When you think of talking to your mom or dad, you get that sick anxious feeling and want to yack.

Perhaps you feel if you don't carry on the family business exactly as your grandfather did, you're failing. And now going to work is making you feel like you're on the edge of constant destruction.

Shall we continue? Your relationship. Fear says you can't be authentic and speak up. Your health. Fear says unless you are in Keto and going to the gym seven days a week, you're fat. Heaven forbid you did something for your health that you enjoy like stretching and walking.

How often do you let fear dictate the terms in your battle?

That's the first thing fear does. It sets up an unreasonable premise and then we do everything in our power to work around that premise in order to win.

I'm telling you this as a pastor, as a friend, and as a fellow anxiety sufferer, sometimes that battle that you're fighting isn't even one that God wants you to enter. Sometimes, there's a better way, a different way. But fear would have you say its fear's way, or no way.

And to that I say, no way.

This idea of fear setting the terms lends itself very well to the next tool that I discovered in fear's toolbox. One that I think you'll know all too well!

Tool #2: Fear Puts A Bad Song On Repeat

I work out a lot.

I know. You're like, "Duh, we can tell. It's fairly obvious when we see you."

It's the one thing I can't hide about myself. People are always asking me if I got a permit for these guns and its difficult finding a shirt that both showcases my sculpted physique and allows me to remain humble and modest.

So, the above may have been a bit of an embellishment, but here's a truth bomb: I sweat. I mean, a lot. It's a family thing. My mom was like that, my siblings are like that. Their children and my children are like that. Evie, my daughter, was playing in the living room last week and I looked over and she was sporting an impressive sweat-stache. I was like "Kid, you're playing with Legos, you're not building the pyramids!"

Gross.

But I sweat. It's difficult for me to find headphones that stay on my sweaty head, and accommodate my freakishly small ears. Seriously, my ears are oddly disproportionate to my head.

I'm starting to get self-conscious now. Anyhoo, the best solution I found while working out was the over-the-ear Beats headphones. And it was perfect because I was at the gym, shredding fat and pumping up the bass at the same time.

Solution, yes! But it posed another problem.

After a couple weeks of using the Beats, I noticed an odor. I thought, wow, this rubber must be defective because I am so sweet, I sweat sugar. As it turns out upon calling Apple, the Beats are neither waterproof nor sweat proof. Under the warranty, I was able to send them back for a small fee and exchange them.

This was a great solution, but yet another problem arose!

They stunk.

I was embarrassed because they stunk. I knew that somehow the odor was going to get permanently connected to my Apple ID and it would be the stigma every time I looked a Genius in the eye at the Apple store.

"Oh, Mr. Linton, we don't serve your stinky small-eared kind in here, sir." He'd definitely have a handlebar mustache, too. Just because.

He'd twist his handlebar mustache and say, "The headphone technician got PTSD from opening up your case."

It's the truth. I can't lie. My Beats stank.

But my problem, as it turns out, is universal. You

also have the same issue. But your Beats stink for a different reason. It's the speaker inside that stinks. I mean, it reeks. I'm sorry to be the one to have to tell you.

You'd be as embarrassed to let people know the thoughts you listen to all day as I would be when that Apple technician opened the FedEx box.

And now we've officially stumbled onto one of anxiety's greatest tools.

You're listening to a negative loop, and it's fueling your fear.

If people could hear your thoughts, what you say to yourself, what you think of yourself, they'd think you're crazy. And further, if you talked to others the way you talk to yourself, you'd go to jail. Seriously, do not pass go, do not collect $200 Martha Stewart would be knitting you a quilt.

Why don't you take a moment and listen to that loop? The sooner you locate the stank, the sooner anxiety uses another tool.

Being a dad to young kids, sometimes I long for listening to old music that I used to. I had some pretty dope playlists, and when my wife and I would go away, we'd listen to audiobooks. Nothing says I love you on a car trip like looking over at your spouse and telling her to shush because you just missed some snappy dialogue from *The Martian*.

Not anymore, though.

Since children, however, the tunes have changed.

The primary music we listen to in our home is in the key of "Daddy Finger", "Brother John", and my personal least favorite, "The Wheels on the Bus".

My daughter went through a phase—though she could barely talk—where she would plead every day all day for Wheels on the Bus to be put on TV. Needless to say, I'm as thankful to Netflix as I am resentful.

And what kind of psycho wants to listen to a two-minute song over and over again? Yikes!

But the song would play over and over and over and over, to the point where I would be on my way to a business event, or to go meet someone at church, and I'm humming it like some sort of deranged man who has lost his mind. I'm rejoicing in the melody as if I just went to a concert the night before and the music stuck in my head.

"Hey Sam, what did you do last night?"

"Dude, I went to this KILLER CONCERT featuring all the hits. It's by a band called *Broken Mental State*. They're more indie than anything. But they brought the house down with their rendition of "The Wheels on the Bus." The crowd went bananas. I mean we *literally* all wet ourselves.

Yeah, I'm being sarcastic. Wheels on the Bus sucks. If you're a parent, you've found yourself in that loop of bad songs more times than you'd like to admit, I'd imagine.

Fear functions the same exact way in your mind.

It puts a bad song, an evil song on repeat in your mind. You hate the song. You hate listening to it. You hate playing it, but every day from sunup to sundown, you're "Wheels on the Bussing" it all the way to unconsciousness. BTW, do you like how I made Wheels on the Bus a verb?

Fear puts a bad song on repeat.

Let's see what Goliath is up to and how true this is as he taunts the nation of Israel.

> "When [they] heard these words of the Philistine, they were dismayed and greatly afraid."
>
> — 1 SAMUEL 17:11, ESV

What did they hear? Well, a lot actually. He taunted them. He taunted their God. He made them fearful because of what he threatened to do with them. But look further.

> "For forty days the Philistine came forward and took his stand, morning and evening."
>
> — 1 SAMUEL 17:16, ESV

The Bible says he took his stand morning and evening. What exactly does that mean? It means that

Goliath got up, stood in the same spot day after day, morning and night, and spewed venomous talk over the nation of Israel. He unsettled them with disgusting pictures of a future that would inevitably be theirs if they would come down and face him.

He tortured them over how weak their God was. He emasculated them by calling attention to their disadvantages compared to his Herculean strength. He was putting them on blast in the morning and in the evening nonstop. What makes this most damning for them isn't the fact that Goliath did this.

But he *repeatedly* did it.

> "...behold, the champion...Goliath by name... spoke the same words as before. And David heard him."
>
> — 1 Samuel 17:23, ESV

When David broke onto the scene, this had already been going on for some time, and David heard him now, but the writer specifically says that he spoke the same words as before.

Wheels on the freaking bus, except with violence, bloodshed and blasphemy thrown in for good measure. These words, not Goliath's combat, kept Israel from advancing toward him.

Not losing a battle, not suffering casualties.

But a bad song. A repeating thought that penetrated even the strongest armor of the nation of Israel.

This is how fear has worked in your life. You have a thought, a recurring thought, and it's a bad thought. It's crippling, it's cumbersome, but it's your theme song.

I'll show you mine.

After having those panic attacks before speaking, I developed a pattern of worrying and thinking about having panic attacks constantly. It was the same thought recurring.

"What if I have a panic attack when I'm speaking. *The church will suffer. I'll lose my professional credibility. I'll hurt people who are already hurting. I'll embarrass myself. If it happens, I will lose my job and I won't be able to provide for my family.*"

Suspend your disbelief. I promise you that those words appeared in some form or fashion every single day for almost nine months straight. Were there times that I didn't hear that in my mind? Absolutely, sure. But there wasn't a day that went by that those words didn't penetrate.

When did it typically happen?

Yep, you guessed it. Morning and Night. First thoughts of the day and the last thoughts at night.

My day was bookended with despair. Anxiety plays some nasty jams and keep in mind that it's a morning person and a night owl.

So, that was the problem. That was the song. It

was nasty, it was dirty, but it was my anthem to anxiety. And guess what...you have one too.

What's yours?

I'm not going to get out of debt ever; this month if I don't have enough money, we won't eat. We'll starve. I'll be a failure as a husband or wife.

My child is so wayward. They're so messed up. I know I'm going to get a call where they are in jail, or dead. I can't bear it so I don't deal with it. If I answer the call or interact with them, I know it will be bad news.

I know my husband is having an affair. If I confront it, my life will end. I know I can't make it without him. I have to let it go. He'll never love me totally anyway.

Some of these songs are more primal in nature. I was counseling a woman from our church once who had a constant fear of dying in public places, and she developed an aversion to going anywhere. Her song went like this.

What if I go to the mall and have a heart attack and die in front of people? They won't save me and I'll die in an embarrassing and gruesome way. Or what if I am at a restaurant and I start choking on my food, what then? I could die at the table alone and no one would save me.

These thoughts have penetrated your spiritual armor. And even if you aren't spiritual, if you're not a Christian, these thoughts have gotten to you. They've broken your ability to reason and they've hindered your ability to make a move.

They've kept you from making that advancement

you need into a battle that you will most likely win. They've kept you from going into the Valley of Elah and seeing what the giant looks like yourself. They've sidelined you.

The bad news is: that's what's happening. The good news: this tactic is one of the oldest ones fear has in its book. Knowing that you're thinking damning thoughts is half the battle to defeating them permanently.

There are tools that you can use to do that. You don't have to keep the demonic wheels on the bus playing. You don't have to. You can fix the mix.

But once you start to adjust the thoughts you're entertaining, don't be surprised when fear puts on a costume party and starts to dress differently to fool you.

Tool #3: Fear Wears A Costume

Kids love when you pretend not to know who or where they are.

Why you ask? I don't know, I'm new to the parenting thing. I think it's cause they're little psychos!

Just kidding, I love my kids.

But my daughter and my son will play a game where they throw a blanket over their heads and walk around taunting me as if I didn't know who they were. Then we play the game.

"Who is it?"

<Giggle, Giggle>

"Who's under there?"

<Giggle, giggle, giggle>

It's cute for the first hundred times for sure.

No seriously, I love the kids.

But fear actually does this quite a bit. And it's yet another tool in fear's toolshed.

Fear wears a costume. Of course it does.

After speaking regularly while constantly dealing with panic, I started to develop another habit: I didn't want to wake up. Monday after preaching, it took every bit of energy to do anything of value. I didn't want to even engage in recreation.

I was exhausted.

I thought it was physiological. It's just my weight, I told myself. I thought it was my eating habits. I thought it was my chrono-type. I'm a wolf, not a rooster. I should be sleeping till noon so I could own the night and howl at the moon.

But it wasn't. Because if I woke up late, I still got drowsy at 9:00 pm.

It was depression. Depression is like anxiety's deadbeat cousin that throws a family party, but invites people to your house knowing that you'll pick up the food bill and the decorations.

My shame grew by leaps and bounds. Now, not only was I experiencing these debilitating panic attacks, but I was sad most times. It wasn't an honorable existence for a "godly man." I was the opposite of what one might expect to find from a "Spirit-Filled" preacher.

Then, I started down a deep path. It's like graduate school for depression. You might have heard of it. It's called hopelessness. Not only did I feel like garbage, but I became utterly convinced that this was probably going to be as good as I would ever feel.

Yeah, folks. Hallmark was beating down my door to get me to craft some wicked poetry.

Roses are red

Violets are blue

Today was real rough

And tomorrow sucks, too.

Just call me the goth version of Maya Angelou.

Did you ever wonder why not only are you anxious, but you're also depressed?

Let's have another look at the David and Goliath story and see how Goliath is doing with this idea and his impact on the nation of Israel.

David had broken onto the scene, and innocently he questioned those serving in the military, including some of his brothers.

"Hey, what's up with this dude? Anyone gonna take a shot, or is he just gonna blaspheme God and make you wet yourself 'til Kingdom come?"

Obviously, a very loose translation. But essentially, he asks what is the plan to deal with this monster and enemy of God. Look at the response of his brother.

> "...Eliab's anger was kindled against David, and he said, "Why have you come down? And with whom have you left those few sheep in the wilderness? I know your presumption and the evil of your heart, for you have come down to see the battle."
>
> — 1 Samuel 17:28, ESV

Listen to the bitterness here.

"Hey whoa, little brother. I know you came all this way, but we have a bigger question. Yeah, this giant is gonna kill us and yeah, the armies are going to be defeated and we are going to be having Philistine culture classes being taught in school, but here's the bigger question: What's going on with them sheep, yo?"

If you don't think this is dumb, you are missing the situation entirely. His brother decides now is the time to discuss David's habits as a shepherd.

Why?

Because he's terrified.

I mean, he is out of his mind with fear. But that's not what you see. Nope, not at all. You see anger. You see rage. You see hate.

Because fear dresses up when it comes to the party, pal (read that in John McLane's voice).

Let me share a little insight about you or maybe some of the people in your life who are angry all the time. You know them. They seem to have a permanent IV drip of Hater Ade.

I promise you, lurking beneath the hard outer shell is fear. Maybe it's a fear that the person they're hurting is going to leave them, so they turn into a big bully to keep them controlled.

Maybe, they are mad all the time, because deep down, they hate themselves and they're afraid that the people they care about are going to have the same opinion of them as they do themselves, so why not just beat them to the punch? Why not just treat everyone like a baby treats a diaper?

Let's move up the spectrum and see a little bit of depression. This one, coming from the top down. The King of Israel, King Saul, God's chosen and appointed man for this battle. David comes to him and says, "Yo King (liberal translation again), what's up with that dude? You gonna light him up or what?"

Saul's response doesn't exactly inspire confidence.

> "And Saul said to David, "You are not able to go against this Philistine to fight with

> him, for you are but a youth, and he has been a man of war from his youth.'"
>
> — 1 Samuel 17:33, ESV

Picture the tone, if you would for a moment. Cue the violin. "Oh David, you naive boy, you could never go against him. You're just a kid, and he's been killing people since he was a kid."

This is not a picture of inspiration and victory.

Remember the movie *Braveheart?* The best scene is where Mel Gibson gets the carnival face paint and says, "They may take away our lives, but they'll never take our freedom!" The soldiers go bonkers. You weren't even Scottish when you saw that, but you got so into it, you looked down and you were wearing a kilt and playing bagpipes! You were Scottish for one moment in time, you trickster!

This speech that Saul gives is the opposite of that.

Saul was depressed. He was hopeless. He was broken. But in the core of the apple of emotional destruction—

We find fear. We see Goliath and that stupid song on repeat.

And we see that fear has single handedly made the nation of Israel run through an American Ninja Warrior obstacle course of emotional sadness.

Is that you? At first, maybe you had panic attacks,

but then, you don't even think of that anymore, do you? You just feel like garbage all the time and life sucks.

You look at your life as if the best of it is behind you. Or the thought of you enjoying what's going on with your family makes you furious. So, you keep them at arm's length.

You're the family hothead.

You're the negative Nelly (apologies if your name actually is Nelly).

You're the one that likes to sleep until two minutes before you have to be somewhere and then be in bed five minutes after you're done.

You figure, less life lived, less pain felt.

Here's the diagnosis: Fear has taken all this from you. Fear has infiltrated your life and masqueraded as other things. You might even be trying to treat these symptoms. Maybe you have Joel Osteen permanently playing on your iPhone on your morning commute.

But you're not missing hope, you're not missing encouragement. Those good things you're trying to add to your life aren't as effective for one reason.

You haven't killed your fear.

Tool #4: Fear Lies

If you don't recognize fear's bad loop, and you have trouble identifying how fear comes to the party dressed as anger, depression, and hopelessness, then I'm going also suggest that you might not really know where fear draws the source of its strength from.

Lies.

Liar, liar, pants on fire.

Yep.

We need to kind of become like Will Farrell when he confronts Santa in Elf (You sit on a throne of lies!).

Lies fuel the fear that grips your life. You may not really buy into that, especially if you've been through a traumatic experience, but it's true. Trauma is an event. A life lived in fear is something altogether different.

The bad mix that kept replaying in my head was that of *what if*. We will deal with "what if" extensively in a later chapter. But I was under the impression that the panic attack I had from the platform would end my ministry. I surmised that the if I went all "mental breakdown" mode while preaching, I would lose everything, including the respect that I had from the congregation.

When my anxiety would come out in conversation, I started to allow those fearful thoughts to cascade into the deeper reservoirs of my self-worth. And I bought everything that fear was selling.

Unfortunately, fear only sells lies.

How do we know Goliath was lying? Am I saying that the giant wasn't dangerous at all?

Nope, not even close to what I'm saying. Most fear has just enough truth in it to green-light it into your psyche. But if something isn't 100% true, it's still a lie. So, let's examine this a little more closely.

> "...Goliath of Gath, whose height was [9 feet, 9 inches]. He had a helmet of bronze on his head, and he was armed with a coat of mail, and the weight of the coat was [126 pounds]. And he had bronze armor on his legs, and a javelin of bronze slung between his shoulders. The shaft of his spear was like a weaver's beam, and his spear's head weighed [15 pounds]."
>
> — 1 SAMUEL 17:4-7, ESV

The writer of 1 Samuel really spares no expense on the details of the Goliath description. In fact, there is more description given to him than any other military person in the Old Testament. It's important to recognize that his armor alone weighed 126 pounds!

When I push my daughter and son up a hill in the stroller, I calculate the added weight to the walk every single time. It's about eighty extra pounds. I feel every single pound, trust me.

Now, imagine if you are a warrior, and you have to add 126 pounds of weight to your body. How agile would you be?

Understand that Goliath is as formidable, for sure. I'm not saying he's not deadly, but he lacks something that David possesses. Agility. You ain't doing American Ninja Warrior with 126 pounds of armor. One time I saw a dude do the ninja course in blue jeans and I almost fainted. Armor that weighs this much is a joke.

But let's take a look a little further on this and see.

"And his shield-bearer went before him."

— 1 Samuel 17:7, ESV

Yes, he had a shield-bearer. Not uncommon at all, but the shield-bearer is mentioned several times in this narrative.

Malcolm Gladwell, the author of a book brilliantly named *David and Goliath,* offers this startling insight into a potential weakness that Goliath has. There is a condition known as acromegaly.

Gladwell asserts that some symptoms of acromegaly include having enlarged growth (inhuman even), and slow motor skills. Another symptom is that of double vision. This may explain why when David approached the giant with his shepherd's staff in hand, Goliath asked why David would come at him with "sticks," plural.

And on top of that, why would this nearly flawless warrior need a shield-bearer. Talk about an easy stinking job.

Shield-bearer comes home and hangs his shield-bearer hat on the hat rack.

"Hey honey, what's for dinner," the shield-bearer asks.

No response.

"Honey, I had a long day, and I wanted dinner."

His wife, a beautiful shield-bearer wife, comes out with her own shield-bearing hat. "You had a long day. I watched you on the GNN (Goliath National News). You literally stood against a stone for the first three hours of the day. Then, you watched YouTube cat videos and you ordered a year's worth of toilet paper on Amazon prime. I have been taking care of these shield-bearer kids all day, and you know their temperaments are very guarded (snicker, snicker)."

Shield-bearer gets up, and grumbles to himself as he goes into the kitchen and prepares a meal with perfectly unblemished hands.

But, if you buy into Gladwell's theory (which I tend to do), that shield-bearer had a big job. He guided Goliath down there and protected him from falling because Goliath needed help.

Now, I preached about this and someone came up and confronted me and said, "What are you implying, that there wasn't a supernatural element to this story?" Then they proceeded to build a fire around me and attempt to burn me at the stake. Since then, I always carry a fire extinguisher and fire-retardant preaching clothes.

Relax, I say. Let's get this straight. It is impossible to imagine a shepherd boy with no military experience and a slingshot to win a war and pull his country from the grips of an undefeatable enemy. Any way you slice it, God had his hand in this thing. However, here's the point I'm trying to make.

Fear is not impenetrable. Heck, it's not even well-guarded. Better still, fear has way less power than we give it credit for.

I'm not going to undercut your feelings. I'm not going to say that when you try to pull air into your lungs during a panic attack and only seem to ingest more panic and worry that it doesn't feel real.

I'm not going to say that your sleepless nights are just you being dramatic.

I'm not going to say that *what if* scenario you keep replaying doesn't have some truth.

But I will stand on the rooftops and proclaim this one fact:

Fear has a weakness. And if fear has a weakness, you better recognize that you can beat it. If you go into this believing that you can win, believing this isn't what God wants for you, believing that you can do better; fear doesn't have a snowball's chance in Maui of making a permanent habitat in your life.

Fear has a weakness. You see its disguise. You see its pattern. You hear that same old song. And you know that sometimes, there is way more sizzle than steak.

Maybe, just maybe, you can let your mind believe and hope once again. Maybe, just maybe you can allow yourself instead of envisioning living like this, that you embrace a life that is free of the shackles of fear.

That's the life I know God wants for me. And I'm going to step out on a limb and say that I believe that God wants that for you, too.

Now, with that being said, since we've come this far, maybe we should step over to our own battle chest. Because, believe it or not, we have some pretty freaking cool weapons to employ to kill fear. We just need to learn how to use them.

PART III
MURDER WEAPONS

"If you are distressed by anything external, the pain is not due to the thing itself, but to your estimate of it; and this you have the power to revoke at any moment."

— Marcus Aurelius

7
GETTING BATTLE-READY

I always get a little wigged out when someone comes to me and says that they heard God tell them something. Don't judge or think I'm unspiritual, but I just feel that way.

I do believe God speaks, and I also believe that God can speak any way He wants. My life has been filled with God speaking to me through his Word, through other Christians, and through sermons and teachings. I know. Sounds very bland, doesn't it? Hey, what can I say?

But God chose to speak to me in a different way during my battle with anxiety. It still sticks with me, and I think if it wasn't for His willingness to intervene, I never would have discovered murder weapons.

I was three months in to my nine-month battle with constant panic attacks. Every time I would step toward the platform at our church, whether it was to pray, preach, or announce a women's dinner, I had a horrible panic attack. I would fight through it, get up and do the speaking, and get off the platform feeling like I just got hit by a Mack truck.

One particular night, three months in, I found myself in a time of intense prayer. I was praying for healing, as I had been. I was praying for deliverance. I was also praying that God would give me some understanding of what was happening.

Up to this moment, I believed those prayers were hitting the ceiling. I'm being authentic here. Of course, I believed that God heard me. Of course, I believed that God was good. But anxiety packed a lunch, and it was wrecking my life. I had begun to see fear as my new normal, and it made my future look incredibly bleak. I couldn't bear the thought of that.

I didn't want to. I would have preferred to quit the church.

It was in that quiet moment of desperation that I felt God spoke to me in my spirit. Not audible. But so specific.

Side note: I believe God often gives us enough wisdom to take the next step. It's beyond the scope of this book, but I always feel bad when Christians say they don't know God's will. I think what they're saying is that they don't know every single aspect of

God's will. That's more like it. But I believe that God gives you enough wisdom for the next step.

This was a time where I felt God told me something specific beyond the scope of the next step. And also, this was how God led me to murder weapons.

Here are the concrete things I heard:

1. Give it a year. That's it. I didn't know what that meant. A year til what? I just didn't know. A year until I resign? A year to be healed? A year before I unload my speaking responsibilities and redouble my focus on ministry elsewhere? No clue. I sympathized with Abram in Ur when God spoke to him and told him just to "go."

But I still was overwhelmed with gratitude to hear from God.

2. Any new speaking opportunity that arose, I should take it. Now, sometimes things are from God and you know it simply by the fact that to you, the idea is inconceivable. That was how I felt about speaking MORE than I already was.

Just the thought of even keeping up with my minimums made me throw up a little in my mouth, but when God challenged me in that quiet meeting to take on anything thrown at me, I felt overwhelmed.

Notice, he didn't say that I had to pursue more, but simply accept more. There is a big difference. And I absolutely wanted to exploit that.

Like when you ask a Christian to get involved in

ministry. They say, "Hmmmm, sounds good, preacher. Can I pray about it?"

"Sure," I say, as I simultaneously make a mental strikethrough on their name in my head. They want God to come down and say just do it. And when He doesn't do that, they warm the bench.

For the first time, I was in that class. God said don't refuse, but He didn't exactly say go pursue. I didn't put an ad in Craigslist saying "Panic Attack Preacher for Hire. He will heavily breathe into your microphone for a modest honorarium."

I didn't do that.

So I found this spiritual prompting both strange, and incomplete as well.

The odd thing about the fact that God laid those convictions on me was how open-ended they were. The year timeframe just made me incredibly uneasy. I felt as though it was possible that maybe God was just going to slowly transition me out of ministry. Or the world was going to end. Hey, I come from a Baptist background. I'm rapture-ready at any given moment, dawg.

And the speaking opportunities, well, that one actually gave me relief. At that time, I was preaching at the church maybe six times per year. I spoke more than a lot of pastors in my position, but not so much that it would paralyze me, as if I were the senior pastor. I did announcements every week, just about. But that was three minutes, as opposed to a mind-numbing thirty-minute sermon which left me mentally broken for at least twenty-four hours after preaching through panic.

I started to think of ways to shirk my limited responsibilities at the platform. I could have some of the volunteers do announcements. I could schedule counseling appointments during church service times. I could purposefully do tech work during those times. God didn't tell me I had to SEEK more opportunities., just not to turn down opportunities.

God is always a little smarter than I am, FYI.

Of course, little did I know that two weeks later, my boss and senior pastor was going to ask me to take over half the preaching schedule...permanently. And that two months after that, I'd be asked to deliver a three-day keynote for a group of eight hundred non-profit healthcare workers.

Sigh. I needed to take Imodium just to relive this part of my story.

But good news for you, I'm going to show you how murder weapons work, so that the next time you have a discussion about anxiety, it'll be to tell your friends how you killed it.

8

WEAPON #1: WRITE WHAT'S RIGHT

I was never much of a journaler. Frankly, I always envisioned people that wrote in their journal each day in a rather comical way.

"Dear Diary, today I am having kind of a gloomy day. I smell the sea in the air and wish I was at the beach, but instead I must pine on and work as through. I am doing a good work and no one notices. Woe to myself."

By the way, this journaler is using a quill pen and he has a small bird in a cage behind him. Just follow the picture okay.

You get the gist.

I never saw a lot of benefit to making that a regular part of my daily routine. I felt like it was easy to become stale and find myself writing just to write.

Until my nine months of hell with anxiety.

The journal became not only my lifeline, but

probably my number one murder weapon of choice on most days. When I am asked by members of the church what got me through, I always tell them there was no silver bullet. Of course, I believe God ordained every aspect of my healing. But frankly, I couldn't imagine achieving that healing without the journal.

So, if anxiety's Crime Scene Investigator (CSI for those that don't watch the show) came to the scene and saw anxiety slumped in the corner, dead and unrecognizable, the investigator would stand up with one of his hands pointing heavenward in a *Eureka* moment and say, "Okay people, an affirmation journal was used here. Find that journal and you'll find the perp!"

Because fear killers write what's right.

Some thoughts before we jump into this section:

I didn't feel the need to start a new, systematic journal. I Googled a bunch of different types of journals to help center my mind. At the end, I made my own. What I'm about to share with you is (mostly) mine. Meaning, I couldn't find one source that featured all of these things.

I didn't write in this journal every single day. Not even close. I gave myself the liberty to write as needed and frankly, that made the difference. Because, perfectionism, yo.

Another thing I learned from listening to Michael Hyatt, a business leader and productivity expert, is that there is scientific data that proves that there is a benefit to handwriting certain things. For instance, I am a pretty fast typist I mean, right now, this keyboard is smoking! Not smoking, like, Pall Mall, but you know what I mean. Michael Hyatt asserts that writing something down with a pen on paper channels a different part of your brain than typing. It forces focus and forces more concentration, and coordination. And focus was what I needed. My mind beat the tar out of me morning and night with anxiety's wicked playlist of hell (see previous chapter).

When I started sitting down, especially on days where panic was especially close to happening, the journal forced me to tell my mind where to go instead of letting fear take the wheel.

Quite frankly, my affirmation journal turned my mind from my worst enemy, to a crucial ally in defeating the battle against fear. Oh, I never told you it was an affirmation journal, did I? Well, I suppose this is as good a time as any to tell you the things that DON'T go in a journal like this. Because these crucial rules are more important than deciding to keep a journal in the first place.

Again, like a diary which records thoughts, my affirmation journal channeled my thoughts. I didn't want to record the thoughts I was having. I already knew my thinking was nasty.

So, here are the things that my JOURNAL WOULD NOT include.

Lies. Yes, everything that went in that journal went through a rigorous eighteen-point detection of falsehood (not quite). But I would not write down things that were untrue. I'll explain this a little further later. But now, as I mentioned, you know those stupid lies that fear tells you. Yeah, I never wrote a thing about those lies. I only wrote what I knew to be true.

Having trouble figuring it out? Good. I'll show you.

If I wrote, "I'm grateful that I didn't ruin the church service with panic."

Here's why that's a lie. I can't control every element of what happens in the church service, and I came to allow myself to believe that even if I had a panic attack while speaking, there's still a chance the service wouldn't be terrible. Lies are like roaches. You see one under your sink, and there is a good chance that a thousand of his friends sent him on a snack run. Have fun sleeping after that illustration!

Hypotheticals. I didn't journal about three years down the line and I'm still struggling with fear as a norm. I didn't put in there, "I pray that I can hide this from my kids so they don't pick it up when they're older."

No, sorry. Hypothetical situations have no business in your journal. I dealt with reality only—that truth at that moment in time. The only time I broke this is when I walked down *What If* avenue. I'll explain what that is later, as well.

What others think. I didn't include this. Not even a little bit. I didn't include what others had to say about my panic attacks or what others said about getting over it. I might have included some things that were affirming and life-giving, but I didn't allow what people thought or what people might have thought to become my barometer for what was included in that journal.

Keep in mind that panic likes to play in a field where the turf is made up of your fear of what others think. You might not be afraid of people, but trust me, shame is keeping fear comfortable in your life. You better serve those folks an eviction notice from your brain if you're going to write what's right and slay the crap out of fear.

Any negative feelings. Nope, I didn't talk about how fearful I was. I didn't talk about how much this sucked. I didn't talk about why I cried myself to sleep the day before, and the day before, and the day before. I kept the journal completely positive. Hence, Affirmation Journal.

If we are being honest with each other, which, I hope by now we are, most diaries, journals, and records of this kind looked like they were written while waiting in line at the DMV with a quill pen (yep, always back to that), in a freezing room, during a dreary rainstorm.

DE - PRESS - ING.

I decided that I wanted to read the affirmation journal as much as I wanted to write in it. Therefore, negativity was gone like a freight train. I had enough negative thoughts flowing through my mind on the reg, that writing them down appealed to me about as much as the salad bar would appeal to Ron Swanson (look it up if you don't like pop culture).

So, what the heck do you write in your affirmation journal? Oh, I'm so glad you asked. Because what we are about to establish may in fact be the turning point in your battle with paralyzing panic and anxiety.

Journal: Truths About God

David Jeremiah said once that the most dangerous lies we tell are the ones we tell ourselves. I can honestly get behind that so much. I'm going to pair that with a paraphrased quote from the great A.W. Tozer who said that what a man thinks about God determines everything about that man.

Put these together and you get this: the most dangerous lies we tell are the lies we tell ourselves about God.

I don't know if you and I are on the same page

with God, but I want you to know I care about you whether you agree with these statements or not. However, let's just set the table with these statements and try to build a framework. Whether you accept these things as true is another discussion all together.

God is perfect. God is good. And God means good for you.

That's all we have to agree on for now. We don't have to debate theology. We don't have to talk about how you were jilted by some church you went to We don't have to examine the intricacies of other religions.

My basis of this idea is simply one word: Jesus.

Jesus died for people that hated Him. Jesus prayed for those that were nailing His hands to a cross. And Jesus had a mission to save those who needed his help. This screams love, devotion, and goodness.

Unfortunately, when we are grappling with things like fear, panic, and depression, our view of God becomes muddy. We use these types of phrases:

- *I feel God has abandoned me.*
- *God isn't working.*
- *God won't answer my prayers.*
- *God is trying to punish me for sins I've committed or that I'm willingly committing now.*

- *Maybe God can't work through this because I'm restricting His power in my life.*
- *I don't know enough about God to ask His help with this.*
- *I haven't done enough to be delivered from this.*

Yes, these are some thoughts that you might be having. If you don't want to acknowledge this, let me do it for you. I was there. I thought these things. Shame didn't stay outside of my spiritual life. When I prayed, I felt faithless, fake, and sinful.

I had studied the Bible for close to two decades when fear crashed my party. I'd been teaching the Bible for almost as long. When you're hurting, your waters of faith are stirred. It's okay. It doesn't make you less. It makes you needy. And we are all needy.

Someone said to D.L. Moody that religion was a crutch. He agreed and said show me one person that isn't limping.

So when the waters of worry erode at your boat (I absolutely love nautical illustrations) you need an anchor (Boom, there it is).

And truth is your anchor.

That's why the first area of my affirmation journal became *Truths About God*.

Let's start this off by saying something we can all agree on: you're thinking of yourself too much.

I say this with humility because I'm with you.

The person grappling with panic isn't worried about the neighbor's car not starting. We are worried about us. I forced my journaling time to center on God first. Why? Well, because God doesn't change. And I was a roller coaster on an unfinished track, bound for destruction and inconsistent in my speed of thought (not nautical, but pretty solid).

Just Him. Just truths about Him. Things that God has chosen to reveal about Himself in the Bible. Again, let's forsake speculation and theological difficulties. Let's instead go with the axioms that most people of faith hold true.

A journal entry might look like this for this section.

- *God is faithful. He doesn't abandon His people.*
- *God looks at us as children, this is why Jesus told us to pray to Him as Father.*
- *God is powerful, always.*
- *God is forgiving, we know this because of Jesus.*
- *God formed the world. He is powerful.*
- *God does miraculous things, sustaining life, producing life, causing the sun to rise.*

Elementary, right?

Not exactly. You remember what Michael Hyatt said about journaling? It creates *focus*. You need it, and if you are having chronic panic, you don't have it.

So, start with some truth or truths about God. If you are a Bible head, you can get deep, as long as it moves you. It has to move you. I'm not talking about letting your emotions lead you, but frankly, as a pastor, I have seen many people mistake Bible knowledge for authenticity with God. Though knowledge helps, sometimes, it's our willingness to know God as Father that we need more than theological tidbits.

If you write something like this:

God has allowed so much continuity between the Old and New Testaments, Jesus becomes the theological key thereby we can interpret both in light of His truth and grace.

That might move you, and if it doesn't great. If it doesn't, get elementary about it. Like a child. Besides, Jesus said that in order to comprehend the Kingdom of Heaven, we must become like children. So, unleash your inner five-year old.

If this makes you mad, tough. You're reading this book because anxiety is stripping you of your joy. Get on your knees, get that journal open, and be moved by the things of God that you know.

Another quick note about why we don't focus on ourselves in this part. Quite frankly, your view of yourself in this situation is very damaged. It's borderline self-abusive. You can't see your way out of it. I said that fear is rooted in lies. Fear lies about us more than it lies about anything.

I speak not out of lack of respect for your mental well-being. This is solely from experience. I found that if I didn't get completely elementary with truth, fear would overcomplicate the things that God made simple about myself and about Him. I had to dumb down this brain (that wasn't terribly difficult) and allow me to believe in the God that loved me first. Making him my "Middle C" with regards to the song that played in my mind—the constant. The One that I could center everything around.

Trust me, we will have plenty of time to talk about ourselves. In fact, let's get a little start on that right now. Now that you you've written some truths about God down, we can expand this and apply it to ourselves.

Journal: Past Victories

Of all of the attacks anxiety had unleashed on my life, the one that plagued me the most was a constant accusation of faithlessness.

Here I was, a pastor, a leader of religious hope. Coming home and grappling with hopelessness like a Pay Per View wrestling match every single week.

I felt like a phony.

But God spoke a word into my heart as I began to

study more about the reality of what was going on in my soul.

I wasn't faithless. I was forgetful.

What's the connection between anxiety and your memory?

Quite a lot, actually. And the affirmation journal gives you the gateway to channel that power.

You see, while you spend so much mental energy fretting about what might happen, you let go of the memory of past victories.

This is a game changer.

How do you recall victories?

Do a brief survey of your life. For me, I looked at this through a spiritual lens. I wanted to see battles that I fought and won under the direction and providence of God.

My thoughts centered around when I lost my mother to an eighteen month battle with cancer. It crushed me, but not as much as the poor choices that I'd made in that period of my life immediately after her death. I was only twenty years old. I thought that I'd gone too far for God's grace.

But God gave me the strength to get back on track. I'll take it a step further—He picked me up and put me on that track.

That's a victory, so I wrote it down.

When I recognized that victory, I recalled another. And another. Pretty soon, those victories were stacking up like board games in your grandma's closet. I had to cut them off. Before I knew it, I had a huge section in this journal that I titled, "Battles I fought and won."

You can come up with your own clever title, and I assure you it will be better. But don't gloss over the importance of this. You need to realize you already have some battles in your win column. You need to understand you are already on the scoreboard.

Anxiety hasn't made you faithless, it's made you forgetful.

Let's look at some potential victories that you can write in your win column.

- Overcoming addiction
- Healing from a relationship gone wrong
- Standing up to a bully
- Financial turn around
- Having the courage to do something good for someone when you didn't feel good
- Entering a job that was challenging
- Losing a job and surviving
- Finishing something
- Staying with something
- Solving a problem

Is this list vague? It absolutely is. And the reason why is because you have to fill in the blanks. Your life has been peppered with a lot of setbacks. Chris Hogan, a financial coach, said that our greatest setbacks are often setups for comebacks. I couldn't agree more.

But you can't forget the good God has done.

How do I know that this was a factor in the David and Goliath story? Did David go to the local Barnes & Noble and find himself a nice leather-bound journal before killing Goliath?

Not quite, but close.

> "But David said to Saul, "Your servant used to keep sheep for his father. And when there came a lion, or a bear, and took a lamb from the flock, I went after him and struck him and delivered it out of his mouth. And if he arose against me, I caught him by his beard and struck him and killed him. Your servant has struck down both lions and bears, and this uncircumcised Philistine shall be like one of them, for he has defied the armies of the living God."
>
> — 1 SAMUEL 17:34–36, ESV

Remember, we talked previously about how David said he had potential to win this battle because he had been slaying animals a long time before Goliath ever brought his tall, ugly face to the battle line.

God delivered him then, and He would deliver him again.

That's the mantra you need to adopt with this part of the journal.

Now, be careful not to pepper the anxiety's bad loop into this. Remember, nothing negative. Don't say, "You gave me victories in the past but I don't know how you're gonna do it this time."

Just stop. For a moment, suspend your disbelief and just focus on those victories and nothing more. Those are tangible things that God brought you through.

Remember, it's a violation of the journal to put negative stuff in there. Right now, I am working with Moleskine on a journal that disintegrates in your hands the moment you write a negative thing and leaves your fingers smelling like onions, stinkbugs (Google them), and cheese.

Yeah, the patent is pending, so let's just be cautious now, shall we?

Speaking of victories we've experienced, we're starting to get more comfortable thinking of ourselves in a positive way. Even if you aren't giving motivational seminars yet, maybe we can advance to Ninja level affirmation with the next section of the journal.

Journal: Truths About Me

Okay, this is the hardest part of the journal you're going to have to do. Not because you don't know your theology. Not because you've tried twice, and the previous two journals disintegrated leaving your hands smelling like kaka. No, this is plain tough. And this took me the longest to do.

But dag gone it, it's important. There, I just Christian swore at you to get you to wake up to this idea.

We can all universally accept that self-worth is a fragile thing these days. Confidence is out the window. In addition to being a pastor, I also am a certified corporate trainer for the Dale Carnegie organization. We specialize in helping people to excel in five key areas that Dale called, "The Five Drivers of Success." One of those areas is self-confidence.

It's mind-blowing how many executives, leaders, laborers, and entrepreneurs have such a difficult time focusing on their own successes. It's astounding, really.

We struggle with self-worth on a regular basis, and it makes sense. We have a God that says in Psalm 139 that we are fearfully and wonderfully made. It stands to reason that we also have an enemy that would prefer to say that we think we were casually and shabbily thrown together.

This next part of the journal is called, "Truths About Me."

Here, I gave myself permission to brag. Not about past victories that God led me through, no. We already covered that ground amiga and amigo.

This portion of the journal deals exclusively with the good things that God has placed into you.

Let me put it more clearly: If someone found your journal and only read this portion, they should get the impression that you are the cockiest human being that ever walked the planet. I mean, they should think that you legit have Tony Robbins permanently playing in your earbuds.

Theological timeout: do I mean that we are perfect? Nope. Do I mean that we aren't sinful? Um, no. But I do believe that God has placed incalculable potential in each human life. You're welcome to disagree with me, but like Adam Sandler in *The Wedding Singer*, I have the microphone. And this is what I will offer.

You're valuable because Jesus died for you. But on top of that, there is value that you bring to the table. Like your past victories, you've forgotten that value. Well, let's pony up and get some of those qualities into this affirmation journal.

How do you do it?

List the things about yourself that you value most.

Pro tip: if you have trouble coming up with

something of value, think about what others that are close to you may have said about you. Look for a pattern or theme.

I'll share some of mine with you. I ain't scared.

- Good public speaker
- Works well with just about everybody
- Driven
- Tenacious
- Funny (um, duh)
- Gifted in encouragement
- Faithful
- Trusted
- Smart
- Motivating

Those are just a few. And this was hard. Now, notice that a lot of mine had to do with areas that fear was attacking. I focused on the fact that I was a good public speaker. How did I validate this? Easy. There are people willing to pay money for me to speak. That's not me saying something I want to be, it's objective. I'm not going to say that I'm a good dancer, because no one has offered me money to dance (yet).

I didn't say I was the best. I didn't say I was better than most, I said I was good at it and that I was gifted in it.

Now, for those of you who might say (though I

don't think there are many) that self-confidence has never been an issue for you, I want to offer a word of caution. Be realistic about what you put in here and not idealistic. Remember, fear messes with you because of lies. Truthfulness is key.

For instance, don't say, "I overcome everything." That's not really true at this point in time because you're still fighting this battle. Or, "I'm not afraid of anything. Fearless about all things." Again, it's idealistic, and it might work well in another context of you claiming a future for yourself but the key here is truth.

I've seen Christians hyper-spiritualize their battles. I've seen them hide behind Christianese and Amens to keep from coming to grips with the pain they were experiencing. Remember, folks, if we are Christians that means we are worshipping the Lord Jesus who asked for the cup to pass from Him in Gethsemane as He was sweating drops of blood from the pressure that He was under (Gospel of Luke, look it up).

Truth is truth. And I heard somewhere once that truth makes you free. So be truthful about the good in you. I'd rather you go overboard. I'd rather you go bonkers and list everything good people have said about you from grade school to now. I'd rather you list the things that you rejoice in about yourself regularly, or perhaps things that fear has left you taking for granted.

Why are we doing this again?

Oh yeah, fear, that's right. You see, you need some focus in your thoughts. Fear is calling the shots because your thoughts are running loose. Remember, it's all about focus. I wish I could tell you that you could control the thoughts that enter your mind, but that's simply not true. You can, however, control what you focus on. If you focus on good things—about yourself, and about God—it's going to yield you a harvest of good output. So, Goliath won't be the only one coming to the table armed with armor. You'll have some of your own.

Oh, and did David do this? Um, yeah pretty much. He did so in his conversation with Saul, and later, we will see that he did it in conversation directly with Goliath. David wasn't afraid to say what he was capable of and the good that God placed in him.

You shouldn't be afraid of that either.

Remember, fear hasn't made you faithless, it's made you forgetful. You've forgotten what you know to be true of God. You've forgotten your past victories. You've forgotten the good in yourself. And you've also forgotten a crucial component of your anxiety arsenal, and it may be the one that fear fears most.

Journal: Promises To Claim

Now that we've distilled the truths about ourselves and God down and topped them with a little bit of past victories, it's time to take what you know of God and the Bible and get offensive. I'm not talking about using potty language. I'm talking about moving in a position to attack. The Bible is described in many ways. One way in the book of Hebrews is as a sword.

Another important application of the Bible definitely merits a look. Jesus, the son God, God in the flesh, used his knowledge of the Word of God to defeat the devil during a temptation in the wilderness after forty days of fasting. See Luke 4:1-12.

That's bonkers to me. He could have done anything, but he used the promises of God. And it worked.

So how do we do this?

The Bible is loaded with promises. Now, as a pastor I'm required to tell you that not all promises are for you. For instance, when God talks about the land that Israel will inhabit in Canaan, that doesn't mean that you can go to Canaan, throw up a bungalow and live off the land in Jesus' name. It does, however, say something about God upholding his promises.

While that caution is important, I believe that most people of faith never truly pursue the promises of God's Word and lay claim to them for their lives.

We tend to look at the Bible as more of an artifact. But I believe God wants you to use it as artillery.

Fear has rooted itself in your mind using lies about yourself, your situation, and about God. Scripture is truth. The truth of Scripture destroys the lies of fear. It's that simple, and that challenging.

I'd like to share with you my "heavy hitters," if you will. These are the ones that I used to help me with fear most. They may not mean as much to you, but seeking God and finding Scriptures that speak to you is worth your investment of time.

> "For God gave us a spirit not of fear but of power and love and self-control."
>
> — 2 Timothy 1:7, ESV

I knew that when Paul was talking here to Timothy, he was reminding him not to be afraid. And God doesn't just say here that you should stop being afraid. He says you should understand you have a Spirit of power and love and self-control.

I was there for that. I needed those things.

Here's another:

> "There is no fear in love, but perfect love casts out fear. For fear has to do with punishment, and whoever fears has not been perfected in love."

— 1 John 4:18, ESV

If I told you I prayed this promise and claimed it out loud one hundred times, that would be a modest understatement. I kept claiming that the love of God expels the darkness of fear in me.

Here goes another:

> "For the gifts and the calling of God are irrevocable."
>
> — Romans 11:29, ESV

Let me explain. I felt as though God had taken away my ability to preach and teach. The Bible describes these as spiritual gifts. When I was at the height of my depression as a result of anxiety, I would cry. It took a counselor to tell me why I cried so much.

She told me I was mourning. I was lamenting the loss of something inside me that I perceived that had died. She couldn't have been more right. I mourned the loss of the experience I had preaching for God and loving my church through encouragement in God's word. It was dead. And I was left in the middle of a burned-out shack that I desperately tried to decorate with denial, apathy, and eventually hatred of myself.

God spoke to me through Romans 11, about the idea that He doesn't take His gifts away. Sure, this is dealing with the call of God in regards to salvation, but the moment you trust Christ, you are given a spiritual gift.

I refused to believe the lie that God revoked my ability to do His work. So every time—I mean every time—I would get up to preach, I claimed that verse.

And just as promised, God's truth killed the lie.

What Scriptures can you include in your affirmation journal? You need to have some keystone panic verses that you use to re-center your mind on truth when it's drifting away in lies. Write them, rewrite them, speak them, and scream them. You have to get to the place when you use the Word of God like Jesus did, as a weapon, not as a decoration.

This isn't about something insightful you say to someone at a church function. This is a battle for your very mind, so you better get used to using that sword. More you do it, easier it becomes. But you have to start. I don't care if it's just two or three verses. But don't blow this off. You do so at your own peril. The truth will make you free and it also kills fear.

And with regards to weapons, there's a final one that should be a part of your affirmation journal. It's more powerful than I can emphasize, but more counter-intuitive than anything we've spoken about yet.

Journal: Gratitude

You feel like garbage and I know it. You wake up hating the fact that you woke up. The thing you fear has become an albatross hanging over your head morning, noon, and night.

All you want is a secret fix, something you can do to feel a little better. A little more normal.

Here is a secret weapon that will surely help you pretty quickly, but you're gonna scoff.

Gratitude.

Okay, seriously, stop scoffing.

Being grateful is a powerful and offensive weapon against fear.

I swear if you scoff again, you're getting throat punched.

No, I didn't mistype.

No, these blue eyes aren't enhanced with tinted contacts. (Just threw that in to see if you were still scoffing.)

Here's the deal. Fear doesn't come just to destroy, but it comes to steal. One of the most valuable arrows in your spiritual quiver is thankfulness of God's work in your life. When we are in pain, when we are constantly battling anxiety, we lose sight of the good that God has already done.

Remember, the enemy uses forgetfulness more than faithlessness. You didn't slam your Bible shut, throw your hands up and profess unbelief to God. But you have forgotten His good work.

So how can we do this? How can we be grateful? What can we be grateful for? And more so, how do we focus on blessing when we feel so broken?

The same way you're doing anything here: Focus. You can't choose the thoughts that enter your mind, but you can choose what you focus on. And the affirmation journal will help you to get that focus needed to be grateful.

Some of the most influential leaders in the world have gratitude as a tool that they use to center themselves and their mind for the day. They may not even believe in God, but gratitude trains your mind to mentally recognize good things that are going on in your life, even if you may be experiencing something bad. We are commanded in the Bible to be thankful in all things, even in bad circumstances.

> "Give thanks in all circumstances; for this is the will of God in Christ Jesus for you."
>
> — 1 Thessalonians 5:18, ESV

If you want to know and do the will of God, one of the simplest things to do is to be thankful.

But if you understood the power of gratitude when fighting anxiety, it wouldn't feel like something you had to do at all, but something you need to do for yourself. Honestly, this isn't busy work, it's a vital component to your battle plan against anxiety.

You see, anxiety steals the conversation. It steals the show. It takes your attention, so even if the greatest thing happens to you in the world, you can't enjoy it.

Because you're destroyed with worry.

So, let's get grateful.

Here are some tips:

First, don't go for the common gratitude grapefruits. You know, those things that most people typically are thankful for. For instance, my family, my kids, my health, my financial stability. Those are all things to be thankful for, absolutely. But I believe that we default to those big-ticket items so quickly that we lose sight of the other things in our lives that we are taking for granted.

Give this a try. Be thankful for three unique things per day.

Here's an example.

I'm thankful for this responsive keyboard I'm typing on. I'm not kidding. I really am practicing that as a part of my gratitude exercise. I'm thankful it's not too cold in my office as I sit and type. I'm also thankful that I just had a huge glass of fizzy water that I made. It really helped wake me up. In a couple minutes, I'm going to be thankful that there is a bathroom two feet from my office.

I'm joking about the bathroom, but not about

everything else. How many little things are you taking for granted in your life? How many opportunities to give God glory for things are you letting slip by. If you prime your mind to be grateful, you'll never tire of thanking God for the blessings He's given you.

Sound stupid? Well, let's put it this way. Those three things that I focused on for thirty seconds here are taking thirty seconds away from fear that it otherwise might have had. When I combine that with writing it down, FORGETABOUTIT! Now you're cooking with gas, folks.

Newsflash: God doesn't need to know what He provided for you for His benefit. He knows because He provided it. But He wants you to know that He provided it. Because when you are thankful, you're acknowledging His provision.

You have to train your brain to recognize good things. All your mind has been doing is focusing on hypothetical situations and bad things. You didn't train it to do that, but you are allowing it to stay that way by drifting toward terrible thoughts.

Gratitude breaks the chains of a mental rut, one link at a time. Every day, journal about three things that you're grateful for. Not just the big things, but the things that might seem insignificant. You're not doing something meaningless, you're doing mental P90X and fear has no place to rest in a mind filled with gratitude.

Now that's a weapon.

Journal Routine Tips

Considering we are asking you to start a journal, I want to give you some quick best practices with dealing with this journal. To emphasize once more how important this was, I had my journal with me almost every time I spoke. I often carried it with me to the platform. It became such a big part of my deliverance from anxiety that I couldn't have imagined not having it.

1. Don't be legalistic about using it. I've seen people really feel like garbage if they don't journal each day. My take on that is that anything that makes you feel like garbage isn't doing you well. I never journaled every day, but there were some weeks where I was more frequent than others.

2. Some things are written daily some things stay the same and you just reflect on them. For instance, your gratitudes should be changing regularly, and you should write new ones. Also, you can always add promises to claim from Scripture and truths about God or yourself. But some of those things may stay the same, and that's okay. Don't feel that you need to add some to each section every day. For instance, you may want to limit truths about yourself (it's hard to do). You may also want to limit past victories to the ones that move you the most.

3.Read it as much as you write in it. Toward the end, I was only updating gratitudes. My journal became more of a guidebook for my battle than an outlet of expression. I would recall specifically the victories that I had won in God and the truths about myself and God out loud. I'll explain more about saying these types of things later. But I don't want you to just write in this and forget what you wrote, I genuinely want you to use what you wrote. Don't make it a once-and-done event. The purpose of the journal is focus, because right now fear is running the show.

Coming to the place where I started using this journal changed everything about how I processed my panic attacks. I don't want you to miss out on a sniper-like opportunity to gain high ground on the enemy. As we talk about advancing, let's dismantle the Trojan Horse of anxiety as we tear apart the two words that are paralyzing you with panic as we speak—

What If.

9

WEAPON #2: WALK DOWN WHAT IF AVENUE

It's the darkest, scariest road you've ever seen, and the Uber driver dropped you there after you'd already given him a review.

There are trees that seem to make a tunnel to the entrance of the road. You can only see about two feet of asphalt. Then, as if your favorite worship leader is led by the Spirit to put on the fog machine, there is a dense cocoon of thick gray fog acting as a barrier of sight to the rest of the street.

The street sign says, "What If Avenue."

You summarily call another Uber. Actually, you grab a Lyft out of spite.

The driver picks you up, and drives.

You don't care where, just as long as you don't have to walk down that road.

We have stumbled onto something that is extremely difficult to understand and even more difficult to apply, but it's one of the greatest potential weapons that you have to go beast mode on fear.

We are going to look at taking a stroll down "What If" avenue. A stroll that most of us won't take because it's too scary. Or even too devastating. But I promise you, if you want to kill fear, you have to do this. And you have to do it sooner rather than later.

At the core of your anxiety, are those two words. What If. The idea of answering that question paralyzes you. It scares you so bad that you just avoid it all together.

But I'm going to tell you how you should get out of that car, and walk down that road. And I'm going to tell you why it's not what you think it is.

Let's consider your first interaction with panic, anxiety, or terror to be your entrance into this evil ride share. Fear doesn't take you where you want to go and leaves no explanation of what it's doing. But then fear does something that stops you in your tracks.

It shows you the worst possible thing.

Well, not exactly.

It shows a potential unknown, and you fill it in with the worst possible thing from your mind. You look down the street and all you see on the other side of the fog is the worst possible outcome. And that is exactly fear's intention.

Fear only forecasts the worst possible outcome,

and because of that we U-turn from the path we should have never left.

And fear wins.

But it doesn't have to be this way.

My "What If"

When I had my first panic attack before performing those baptisms, I made a bad mental bookmark.

From that point on, I was riddled with several recurring thoughts.

What if this happens when I'm preaching?

What if I get winded and become so embarrassed by this that I can't talk?

What if people realize how mentally ill I am?

Those what ifs always led me to darker scenarios. Public embarrassment, shame, guilt, and the loss of my job. All of this became a trail mix that fear made for me to digest mentally for nine months straight.

It. Sucked.

I'm going to say that you have the same thing going on. You have looked at What If Avenue, and you've chosen, just like me, that it's better to let fear drive you where it wants to go.

But I'm going to make this crazy suggestion, what if, what if...

What if you got out of that car, and stepped on to What If Avenue on your own?

What would happen?

Well, I'll tell you. You'd freaking kill fear, that's what.

Goliath's What If

Let's get back to Goliath and see how he mastered What If Avenue. And boy, did he ever.

Goliath stands, taunting David—this young man who stands in the valley looking up at him. He paints this very vivid picture.

And it is the worst possible picture.

> "...The Philistine said to David, 'Come to me, and *I will* give your flesh to the birds of the air and to the beasts of the field.'"
>
> — 1 Samuel 17:43–44, ESV, emphasis mine

Now, don't let this be lost on your 21st century mind. David was a good, obedient Hebrew. Just about the worst possible thing that could happen to someone like him would be to die without being given a proper burial. I mean, that was the worst possible scenario.

If you don't believe me, read Exodus, Leviticus and Deuteronomy with regards to burial of the dead. The fact that this uncircumcised giant was going to kill David and let his body rot in the open was not only a bad outcome, but the worst that could be. It inspired fear in any Hebrew heart.

But we forget what this statement is.

It's a hypothetical. It hasn't happened yet.

Friend, this is one of the greatest tricks of fear.

Fear always says, "The worst possible thing will happen."

My Trip Down "What If Avenue"

We have to spend a good bit of time on this particular *what if*, because it encompasses so much of what we think.

What if other people think less of me? Or maybe, what if I embarrass myself in front of other people?

I wish I could tell you as a thought leader for a spiritual organization that I do not get moved by the opinions of others. I wish I could see that my internal resolve is as steely as Superman's exterior and that nothing penetrates me, but after close to fifteen years of ministry, I still worry about failing in front of people.

And fear took this worry and ran with it for nine months.

Anxiety loves to get others involved and make your personal and mental well-being a team sport: except anxiety recruits everyone else you know to its team.

What a jerk move!

Weapon #2: Walk Down What If Avenue | 151

When I had my first panic attack, it took place in front of a board member, a baptism coordinator, and the entire worship team. These are people I ministered to for years. I buried some of their family members, counseled them through divorces, and even was there when some of them had babies.

In a moment, that connection was severed as I became the one that was in need. And by "in need" I mean, powerless, helpless, and hopelessly relying on their support to get me through those moments where I couldn't do what I had to do.

It was the most humbling, and embarrassing thing I'd ever experienced.

Not only that, I felt shame. This inward shame at what they must be thinking. I thought of them losing faith because the pastor that was teaching them faith is now faithless. Yes, how gross is that self-talk? I viewed going through anxiety as faithlessness.

Do you see what fear does? Do you see how fear forces you to accept its own definitions as universal?

Either way, I felt I was letting them down. And a deeper cold wave of concern came upon me, and this I couldn't shake:

What if my existence at the church is hurting the church?

I can't say I felt like this every time, but it was pretty regularly after having panic attacks and hiding in the side room before speaking. It became such regular part of my thinking. It took a trained Christian psychologist to pull it out of my psyche, like an infection being treated by a doctor. It had set in so deep.

I sat on her couch, and she asked me what I was worried about happening.

"I'm worried I'll hurt them."

"Hurt who?" She asked.

"The church people, the leaders, the members." I could feel the shame.

"How?" she asked.

The baptismal coordinator's words floated to my mind. "If something like this happens to you, what does that mean for us?"

"Well?" She asked patiently.

"Well what?"

"Did you ever answer the question?" She sat waiting for me, knowing that I never had.

"What do you—I mean, yeah, I would hurt them." More shame. More pressure. It was a buffet for fear in my head.

"Let's do this, let's pretend that it happens, right in the middle of your preaching. Let's pretend you experienced a panic attack that's so bad, so horrible that you can't speak. How long do your panic attacks last, typically?"

"I would say, well, maybe thirty seconds. Maybe. But it depends on where I am. Sometimes they're shorter."

She smiled, "Good, so we have a frame of reference. Let's go to a sermon. You have a panic attack, it lasts for thirty seconds, what happens?"

"I hurt the church and I—"

This time she interrupted, "No, I mean what instantly happens, take me to the scenario, what would happen in the moment, not the implications you think would happen."

I had never done this. "I would say, I need a moment, and step to the side."

"Okay, so you would step to the side. What would happen next?"

This was hard for me to envision. "I would either have another pastor come up and finish the service, or an elder."

"No, you wouldn't really do that, would you?" She knew I wouldn't.

"Well, yeah?"

"No, it's only thirty seconds. People are tortured for longer than thirty seconds. Anyone can last thirty seconds. What would happen next?"

I was starting to visualize having the panic attack under her direction. She made me close my eyes and recreate the scenario, same players, same night, same panic. I'm late, my heart races.

"Go ahead, what would happen next?"

My mind was misfiring, the pictures that I had focused on suddenly became blurry and I started to see a new picture, a foreign one.

"I would make a joke or something." I knew this to be true.

"Of course you would. And then what would you do?"

"I would finish."

"Yes, but let's say you couldn't, let's say it did get so bad that you had to step away."

"Another pastor would come and conclude the service."

"Would you lose your job?"

"No," I answered so confidently. I knew that I wouldn't lose my job over this.

"What about the people, what are they doing?"

Fear asserted itself. "They're hurt because—"

Forcefully, "No, listen, think about them. Think about what happened during the panic attack, what did they do after. Immediately, what happened. Not what you might do, but think about what happened. Focus on the room."

For the first time since the panic attack, the picture in my mind changed. I remembered them waiting for me, and I remembered them asking me if I was okay. I remembered how my friend's hand felt on my shoulder. I remember how the board member came to my office after and asked me if I was okay.

I started to remember other things. I remembered laughter that we had before. I remembered the relationships I had with them. All their tragedies and triumphs. All the ups and downs.

I remembered their love.

And suddenly, I was crying. I cried and cried. A wave of relief spread over the burning pain in my mind like a freezing rain. I remembered happy moments, and I remembered tragic moments. But I remember that I was there. And the size of the panic shrunk. It became almost impotent under the size of the magnitude of the rapport I'd built with a lot of these men and women.

Then, it began to extend out into the congregation. I visualized them instead of being judgmental of me, standing beside me. Helping me.

Maybe even loving me.

The emotion of this exercise goes beyond this description.

But this was the turning point. This is when I realized that What If Avenue has some dark spots, but it's not as dark as it appears.

What if I had a panic attack? Well, maybe they'd help me. Maybe I'd be needy. And maybe, I'd be all the better for it.

Take Your Own Walk

Have you ever followed it? Have you ever walked down and let the streetlights come on? What if what you fear is more tragic?

What if you're afraid of losing that loved one?

What if you're afraid of getting that call that every parent dreads?

I'm going to suggest this to you. Some things are tragic, and we can't think about them. Some things are tragic and we shouldn't think about them.

One person in particular told me once, that they viewed it this way. They have to do what they can when they can. But at the end of the day, they can't control what's going to happen with that child whether they're fearful or not. Now, this may sound cavalier and even dismissive, but keep in mind it took this person almost five years to reach this place.

The fact is we don't know what that picture is like on the other side of what if. We are going to experience bad things, but Jesus said that we wouldn't be alone. He promised in this world, we would face tribulation, but he also stated plainly that he has overcome the world (John 16:33).

I don't know what your picture is, but can you let God change it? Can you see things not going as badly as you plan? Can you maybe, just maybe, walk down that road and refuse to climb back into fear's car?

As I sat in that counselor's chair many times over the nine months that anxiety gripped me, I told her I didn't want to experience this. I told her that I didn't want to go through this.

But when it comes to getting your head out of what if, the only way out is through. Really distill down what would happen as an immediate result of your panic attack. Also, ask yourself, how much hypothetical have I allowed fear to pass off as fact.

If you can train your brain to take the trip, maybe the lights on that road will become bright enough to walk, albeit slowly. And maybe, just maybe, you will be able to move a little faster.

And maybe, you can get to the other side. I did. And there is no reason why you can't. But you have to talk yourself through it. Because fear is all talk. And if you want to kill it, we have to examine how you need to talk a little more.

10

WEAPON #3: TALK TO FEAR MORE

We've done some writing, we've done some walking, but now it's time to do some talking.

Perhaps one of the greatest hidden ways that anxiety dominates our lives is the way it dominates our conversations. Especially with regards to discussing it with others.

I've spoken to many people over the years that struggle with chronic anxiety or bad thoughts, and frankly, they wear it on their clothing like a name tag at a class reunion. You know, the reunion you went to where NO ONE looks like they did in high school. You stop and ask yourself if others are thinking that way about you.

If anxiety creeps into all of your conversations, it's only a matter of time before it creeps into your identity.

You know people that this has happened to. Hey, you may even be one of those people.

They'll say things like, "Oh, goodness, I can't do something like that. My anxiety, I can't even..."

Now, I am aware that most times this is just joking, or maybe it's something you just say to get someone off your case about something. But no one can deny that when anxiety or any mental stressor becomes a part of your conversation, it dominates.

How could I do that, my anxiety?

My OCD is kicking in, I'd never be able to travel.

I was in my boss' office, and my legs where shaking because of my panic attacks.

Listen, anxiety is not a purse dog. It shouldn't be something you carry around.

I'd be more for a purse dog than anxiety.

We have an eight-pound Shih Tzu Bichon mix, You could put her in a large McDonald's bag (not that I would do that, don't call Sarah McLachlan).

That's cute to have a purse dog.

Having anxiety be the center piece of your conversation with people isn't.

I talked about it, but minimally.

When I was about to do any type of speaking, my secretary would say, "How's the pan..."

I would stop her mid-sentence, as if she were saying Beetlejuice's name for the third time (once again, Google is your friend, young ones), or Bloody

Mary's name in the bathroom mirror. I didn't want it to be the topic.

I wasn't in denial, like I was in before, but this was conscious conversation control.

I never said, "my anxiety" because I don't want this thing to feel comfortable being a part of my scene. I want it to feel as uncomfortable as you do when someone notices you're wearing pajama bottoms when you ran out to get something to eat. Not that something like this ever happened to me. I read it on a blog or something.

But how often do you use words like "my anxiety" or my "panic stuff," or "my OCD."

It's not yours. It's not meant to be yours. You're talking like that because you are trying to be comfortable with something you simply weren't designed to ever be comfortable with. But not only do you have to limit how much you let panic consume your conversation, you also have to control the conversation with fear itself.

David Speaks Up

More pressing than the conversation anxiety consumes is the conversation it has with you. We touched on this earlier when we said that panic plays a bad song on repeat (day and night) in your mind.

Let's examine this in the Goliath story.

> "...The Philistine said to David, 'Come to me, and I will give your flesh to the birds of the air and to the beasts of the field.'"
>
> — 1 Samuel 17:43–44, ESV

As we said, this would have been the absolute worst thing in the life of an obedient Hebrew like David.

But notice the number of words Goliath speaks to David here. If you count the Hebrew (let's just do that so that we can keep it consistent) it's just above twenty words plus a non-recorded cursing. Let's say maybe thirty to be generous. Those words would have absolutely terrified even the most faithful of the people of Israel.

Those thirty words are more intimidating than anything, for sure. And right now, the loop in your head may be less words than that. Mine was "I'm going to have a panic attack on stage." Or "I'm going to embarrass myself." Or "I'm hurting the church."

Those few words were paralyzing.

David's response when viewed through this lens is crucial to killing fear.

> "Then David said to the Philistine, 'You come to me with a sword and with a spear and with a javelin, but I come to you in the name of the Lord of hosts, the God of the

armies of Israel, whom you have defied. This day the Lord will deliver you into my hand, and I will strike you down and cut off your head. And I will give the dead bodies of the host of the Philistines this day to the birds of the air and to the wild beasts of the earth, that all the earth may know that there is a God in Israel.'"

— 1 SAMUEL 17:45-46, ESV

In the Hebrew, David speaks to Goliath. using over 90 words. That's over three times more words than Goliath. Herein lies the secret.

You have to speak to fear more than fear speaks to you.

It's just that simple. You have to be willing to talk over the talk that's overtaken your mind. You have to be willing to shout into the darkness the truth of light. Let's see how to do this.

Faith-Filled Self-Talk

I didn't pick this principle up until about midway through my battle with anxiety, but when I realized the power of this, I never stopped.

The back room, where I initially had my first panic attack, had become the battle ground before each time I spoke. It had turned into a place of absolute dread. The interesting thing about that area is that it's completely private. No one goes back there unless there is an emergency or they are getting off stage, so I began to experiment with self-talk.

Out loud. To myself.

Now, hear me on this. I was talking. Out loud. To myself. That may seem insane, and if you would have witnessed me doing this, perhaps you would have felt the same. Perhaps you would have told me that I need to see someone, to which I would have responded by telling you to get out of my face, I already am seeing someone.

But here is the power.

Anxiety comes at you with the same thoughts. Morning and night. Morning and night. Day after day. It starts and ends with a chorus of evil murmurings that terminate in your lack of consciousness at night (if at all, because I dreamt of the things that I feared, as well).

So I decided to respond.

There are times where when I felt myself about to go into a panic attack and I would stop. I would lift my face up, pull my shoulders back, and simply say, "No."

Or I would say, "I'm not afraid of this." Or "I love this."

It started off small. Just those elementary murmurings. But then, it increased. "I'm not going to allow fear to stop me from something I'm called to do." Or "I'm stronger than fear because of Jesus."

But let me tell you what put this practice on steroids.

I began to take my affirmation journal (told you this came in handy) and speak out loud those notes that I had of past victories, those thoughts about God, those promises to claim and even, yes, the truths about myself. The content of the journal morphed into a verbal ammunition that I would aim toward fear in the silence.

I would stand there and say, "God has equipped me for this, the gifts and calling of God are irrevocable (Romans 11:29), and God has not desired to take away what he has gifted me to do."

Yeah, that's just one. Now, if you came into the backroom, you'd think I was out of my gourd crazy!

Whoa, look at him, now he's preaching to the dust mites!

But I didn't care. I could tangibly feel fear retreating, be it ever so slightly. But there was something else going on here that shouldn't be ignored.

I was controlling my focus. Instead of letting fear dominate my mind, I was channeling myself to get to the place where fear became a target, and I was set to annihilate it with faith-filled self-talk.

Now, it's your turn. Stop talking about anxiety and start talking to it. Stop panicking and start preaching. Stop letting the lies fear has laid down be the soundtrack of your sorrow. Fear has come at you with falsehoods and lies, but you came at it in the name of the living God.

You have your victories in mind, you know who you are, you know what God has done for you, you know who He is. You are locked and loaded, as they say. The murder weapons are in your go-bag. So let's not just sit here admiring them.

It's time to do what most will never do with anxiety.

It's time to schedule the battles.

PART IV

DEAL THE DEATH BLOW

"You gain strength, courage, and confidence by every experience in which you really stop to look fear in the face... You must do the thing which you think you cannot do."

— Eleanor Roosevelt

11

MAKE YOUR MOVE

When you think you finally get used to something only to realize you're not further along—that just sucks.

Each time I spoke, I felt overwhelmed after with a discouragement that surpassed anything I'd ever felt. When people told me they enjoyed the sermons, I felt like I was being fake. Each word I spoke was laced with the poisonous presence of anxiety.

I thought maybe I was turning a corner. Maybe the preaching was wearing away at anxiety. And maybe, I'd start to normalize.

And then I received a call. A call that was from God and a call that I didn't want to answer.

Someone on staff was connected to a local non-profit organization related to healthcare. As I mentioned earlier, they had roughly eight hundred team members and they were having trouble securing a keynote speaker for a three-day training seminar. Turns out one of the leaders went online, looked at some of my sermons, and thought I might be a fit.

When they called me, I had the opportunity, the golden opportunity right there to say no. I could have just said I was busy that day. But I honestly felt as though the Holy Spirit opened my mouth and made a yes come out. It was pretty horrible. It tasted like vomit.

I agreed. Three days. Eight hundred people. A one-hour motivational speech. Not a sermon. Not a meeting. Straight up motivation.

The same week, a pastor friend of mine asked if I would preach at his church at the beginning of August (exactly one week before the keynote). Same deal, I said yes, of course. Why wouldn't I? As I cried and wet myself.

This conversation took place at the beginning of June. I thought, well, at least I haven't been as panicked. Maybe this is me turning a corner. Maybe this is me getting tougher. Maybe I won't even be anxious.

But I was dead wrong.

The last three months of June to August would prove to be the most difficult in ministry I ever had.

All the exercises that I'd been doing, the affirmation journal, the gratitudes, the Scriptures—I was doing it all, but fear called out for reinforcements.

The reason why is clear in hindsight. I was coming close to the end. Fear and I were in the ring. The bell sounded. We'd been sparring, but now, it was getting personal.

In June I knew one thing. Either by the end of August, I would be free from anxiety, or it would win. Two of us went into the ring, but only one of us was coming out.

When Fear Knows You're Fighting

I can't speak to your situation at all, but I know something that's universal.

Fear doesn't want you to fight. Fear wants you to let it go and to accommodate it as you've always done. Fear doesn't want you to read this book.

Fear doesn't like when you make progress. Fear doesn't like when you understand how it works.

I know this, because the moment I started to gain a little momentum to overtake fear, it called for back-up.

Here is my encouragement: if it's getting harder, that means your're on the right track. If the path seems darker, that means the next corner you turn may lead to light. If you're in pain, that means that relief is right on the other side.

My counselor told me something mid-July, as I

sat in her office, crying because my panic attacks had become worse.

I started having them when I was visiting people. I started having them when I would speak at meetings of three people. I started having them when I was going into corporate trainings that I had been doing. I had one when I was doing a real estate transaction.

Panic had become a way of life, the depression increased and my desire to do anything decreased.

The counselor told me that the only way out was through.

I didn't want to hear that.

I wanted her to tell me that God was going to heal me.

I asked if she thought I would ever have a panic attack during a sermon.

She said, most likely, yes.

And that had never happened. My attacks came before and I powered through it. As soon as I started speaking, it went away. So as my panic attacks elsewhere increased, I became increasingly nervous that anxiety was going to invade my sermon like church goers invade the Golden Corral Sundays at 1:00.

And she was right.

One Sunday in July, I started into a panic attack during the sermon, and it didn't end. I couldn't breathe, I became foggy, I started to think I was lightheaded.

I was panicked. I powered through the sermon, finishing a little early. When I got off the stage, I felt like I was going to pass out.

Hanging over me was this keynote speech (three days, one hour per day) and speaking at another church. Every time I thought of these events, I had a panic attack.

Fear knew I was fighting, and it started playing dirty.

And that's when I made the decision to deal the death blow. I didn't quite know what that meant at the time. But I was on the edge of finding out.

Step 1: Move Quickly And Constantly

I want to encourage you that if you feel anxiety is increasing as you're applying these things, you're probably on the right track.

Remember, fear deals in lies and deception. Not truth. So the deception here is that if you try to remove the anxiety that has permanently nestled itself into your routines, you will experience more fear. From a value proposition perspective, it's simply not worth it.

There's truth here. You will experience some more fear. For sure. But you must understand that it's worth it.

As one person who struggled with anxiety to another, the life I was living, even with the anxiety being at bay, wasn't a life I ever wanted to live. Never in my wildest dreams would I imagine sitting at a venue ninety minutes before I was supposed to speak, because I had an unrealistic fear of being late.

Never would I imagine that if I was going to lead a meeting, I would have to designate someone to open the meeting up for me just on the chance that I would have a panic attack.

That's not a life for me. It's not for you, either. I know it. You know it. Fear knows it.

And fear also knows that you can kill it.

Goliath knew he wasn't impenetrable, as well.

And so did David.

Was it scary? Yeah, it's a little scary. Look at someone that's twice your size and wants to kill you. It's a little intimidating.

And David does something unique as we see the dealing of the death blow unfold. And that's what we are going to explore for the remaining part of the book. Pay attention to what David says to Goliath before the attack.

> "And David said, "The Lord who delivered me…will deliver me…"
>
> — 1 Samuel 17:37, ESV

Again, David reframed his current battle in the context of God's deliverance. He used the remembrance of the lion and the bear, and he focuses not on his ability, but God's providence in those intense victories. I wonder if there is a place where you can recall your past victories quickly (Hint: it's in your affirmation journal).

The Lord who delivered me, will deliver me.

Can you say that again? Well, let me ask you this question instead.

Do you think God only can deliver you so much? Do you think he gets tired of delivering you? Is his deliverance like an MTA card in New York City— only so many trips? Do you think that He's delivered you from enough and now He has to spread that deliverance around like Nutella at a staff meeting: sparingly?

I don't think so. I think that God specializes in deliverance. I think God loves when people are in situations that they couldn't get out of without Him. He delivers us to remind everyone tangibly of His power.

The Lord who delivered me, will deliver me.

Deliverance isn't just a one-time event. Deliverance is a part of who God is. He is a deliverer.

David looked at his win column, then he looked at the God that gave him the wins.

You should, too.

We asked you this already, but what has God healed in your life? What has God allowed you to come through? Think of time when you felt God's hand, and how he pulled you from the grips of something that was otherwise impassable.

You know it's the same God, right?

The God of your past victory is the same God in your present valley.

Yeah, God's power doesn't decrease over time, like your kid's ability to listen as the day goes further toward bedtime. His power isn't like a battery. It's always readily available to Him.

You need to tap into that and recognize that this battle is already won in the spiritual level.

> "...For the battle is the LORD's, and he will give you into our hand."
>
> — 1 Samuel 17:47, ESV

I checked the scorecard, and Jehovah is undefeated. Let him fight for you.

Get yourself mentally and emotionally ready to accept what God has already done spiritually.

If God killed death through Jesus, He can kill your fear as well. So, let's get moving, because movement is the key if you want to deal the deathblow.

You're Going To Want To Run Away

I stood getting ready for the upcoming keynote, in the middle of a Barnes & Noble Cafe. Maybe because I've always wanted to be a writer, drinking coffee in this bookstore makes me feel like Superman in his Fortress of Solitude. Except with no tights and not as many abs.

I remember sitting there at the keyboard of my computer, looking down at my notes for the talk, and having mini panic attacks every time I imagined giving the keynote. Though I had already spoken at the church a couple dozen times recently, through panic, my anxiety was ramping up. I felt like this was it.

I got a call from the coordinator of my keynote; they talked to me about the tech expectations and asked me about my talk. They said is everything still good with my coming.

I froze in my chair. Listening to them ask that question brought about the greatest temptation. I had nothing to lose by saying no. I had nothing to lose by simply saying I was sick, or something came up, or heck, I'm having panic attacks and I'm not the best for your eight hundred leaders.

Sure, I would lose credibility with them, but the consequences would be absolutely minimal. These people don't know me. They don't go to my church. I can call this off.

"Is everything still good, Sam?" the administrative powerhouse who organized the event asked.

I didn't realize right then, but I was being tempted to turn around. It wasn't God giving me an out, it was the devil trying to get me to turn my back on something that God was trying to do.

It was, enticing, to say the least.

"I'm good," I said, while swallowing the words I really wanted to say.

There is no silver bullet to this panic attack stuff. Fear doesn't respond to your shortcuts. You gotta keep moving, but if I could tell you one thing that saved me time, heartache, and pain with anxiety, it was the way I answered that call. It really was. And it all clicked. Why God told me to take more opportunities. Why God told me never to say no. It was simple.

You have to move quickly and constantly toward that which you fear.

That sounds so absolutely counterintuitive. But as I said, the worst thing I did in the beginning was trying to delegate my speaking.

We do that all the time. But that's letting fear have the day off. If I was gonna go into a panic attack, I was gonna make fear work for it.

David did this. And this is what we saw in the beginning.

> "When the Philistine arose and came and drew near to meet David, *David ran quickly toward the battle line to meet the Philistine.*"

— 1 Samuel 17:48, ESV, emphasis mine

Goliath stands up, and that's where all the armies of Israel shuddered. They couldn't believe it. He wasn't as big as they thought he was.

He was bigger.

His spear was sharper. His face was darker. He was pure evil.

But here comes this short guy, running toward him, like a Hebrew Kamikaze. They probably felt bad for him. Some of them probably laughed at him. Some of them probably cried for him.

But he was the only one who felt free. Because he wasn't alone. He was running with God. And God was about to do something

You have to move quickly and constantly toward that which you fear. You can't retreat. You can't stop. If you stop, you're going to stay that way until you die. I don't have much time left with you, so I'm going to be as blunt as possible. Just as blunt as my grandma was when I came downstairs one Christmas and she said, "Wow, Sammy, you got fat."

Thanks, Grandma.

You'll get used to the fear. You'll accommodate anxiety. You'll be the hoarder, you'll be the person who has built a house around fear's bad habits, and you'll be the one that loses yourself in the valley of fear.

I believe David running toward Goliath was a moment of total self-forgetfulness. I believe he recognized that this was one of the biggest things he would ever do.

Repeated exposure to what you fear removes its power. That's why you have to keep moving. That's why you have to book that trip. That's why you have to have that conversation. That's why you have to start that business. That's why you have to quit letting fear tell you how it's going to go.

I didn't realize every time I spoke, even to do announcements, I was slowly taking pebble by pebble away from the wall that fear had built to keep me from where God had wanted me to be. I didn't realize that in putting myself in a position of vulnerability, I received a victory, albeit small.

The more you turn from fear, it grows. The Israelites didn't understand that, but David did.

I closed my laptop at the Barnes & Noble. I was done with the presentation on paper. Now I just had to do it. I was getting ready also to speak at a friend's church. Both of these foreign things were plaguing me.

I was about to go for the main event. Fear had already arrived at the arena. But there was one thing left I had to learn. And that, is Step 2.

12

ADVANCE MORE THAN ONCE

The first main event happened at a friend's church. It was a small group. A small setting. But I wasn't used to playing outside of my pond.

I walked into the sanctuary, and panic gripped me as it had for the past eight months. I got up, struggled to get my breath, and fought through a sermon in front of strangers.

Again, I left there feeling exhausted, beaten, and depressed. Again, I worried about the big speaking engagement coming up. A three-day keynote to eight hundred members of a non-profit organization.

I was coming completely to the end of my ability to manage this. But I had this little victory. And I thought because I was able to preach in a foreign area, that would be enough.

But it wasn't.

No one tells you you're going to have to move on

fear more than once. But it's threaded into the Goliath narrative. It's worth taking a look at.

> "And David...took out a stone and slung it and struck the Philistine on his forehead. The stone sank into his forehead, and he fell on his face to the ground."
>
> — 1 Samuel 17:49, ESV

Yessssss. This is the moment in church every preacher loves to preach. David kills the enemy of God. David slays the giant. David conquers fear in the valley of fear.

We want to ignore the forty days it took them to get there, yeah. We want to ignore the nation of Israel's weakened state because they'd accommodated the giant's taunts. We want that stone in the head. And almost no one, I mean no one, talks about what happens next.

See, while David hit him with a slingshot, there was something else going on. David was exercising a plan he had the whole time. We talked in the beginning how Goliath demanded a victory by combat situation. Convenient, considering there was no one in the land big enough to make this a match worth fighting.

David never accepted the terms. David wasn't a hand-to-hand combat kind of guy. David was a slinger. And there is a good chance that the stone that came from his sling topped out around forty-five miles per hour. It was comparable to taking a gun and shooting someone at point blank range.

In terms of battle strategy, Goliath was a giant sitting duck.

David did what he knew to win a battle that won the war.

Insert William Wallace scream here, but not so fast.

There's one other thing we see happen in this story.

> "Then David ran and stood over the Philistine and took his sword and drew it out of its sheath and killed him and cut off his head with it."
>
> — 1 SAMUEL 17:51, ESV

Yeah, David ran once more toward Goliath. One more time. Now, if it were me, I would have had my Uber Camel driver get me out of Elah quicker than you could imagine. I would have ditched the slingshot, and been outta there.

"Yo, folks, tomorrow, let me know if he stayed dead."

But David saw the same movies I did, metaphorically speaking. And he knew that fear wouldn't stay dead. So he took the option out of the equation completely.

In my opinion, this is where David shined most in the story. He advanced again. Surrounded by the enemies of God. Surrounded by the disillusioned Israel Army.

David then decapitated the enemy that haunted his entire nation with the giant's own sword. What a remarkable feat of Beastmode.

Step 2: Advance More Than Once

Fear wants you to only get through it once, but killing it involves repeated advancement.

Sorry, Charlie. We didn't come this far to not be truthful with one another. You may have had a good day being in public with social anxiety knocking on the door, but tomorrow's another day. So keep advancing.

You may have dealt with those finances and balanced your checkbook for May, but June is next month, so keep advancing.

There are trains to ride on. Elevators to board. Boats to sail on. And oceans to wade into. Everything good is on the other side of fear. And just like David, you have to advance more than once to stake your claim to the victory that's already, ironically, been won for you by God.

Have you reached a point with fear where you

Advance More Than Once | 185

feel like fighting is no longer worth it? Have you reached a point where you've completely abandoned the idea of a confident life?

That's the worst. The Bible talks about how hope that is deferred makes the heart sick. And heartsickness is a dark place. Picture fear being a toxin that attacks your mind. You have a panic attack, a sleepless night, or an anxious conversation.

After about 1000 of those, it starts to travel elsewhere through your nervous system.

Like you, I viewed my entire life through the lens of fear. And I knew that even though one speaking event was under my belt, I had the biggest one of my career.

And with regards to my sanity, the most important event of my life.

When I got there, there were hundreds gathered in the main meeting hall. They were tired from lunch and a day of lectures (the perfect place for a keynote speaker to go). Talk about adding fuel to the fire! It's scary to know that you are the one thing keeping people from going to their cars and families at a mandatory event.

But I digress.

The moments before giving my first speech were foggy for me at best. My heart was pounding out of my chest. I gripped my affirmation journal to my side. I didn't need to open it. I had memorized what was in there. I heard entrance music, the lights to the stage lifted on, the crowd applauded.

And I took another nineteen steps.

Different Tears

For three days I delivered a motivational speech. For three days, the speech didn't go as I expected.

It went better.

The first time I got in the car after delivering the first of three, I was in rush hour traffic coming back to the city where I live. I have never been so happy in traffic. I was screaming, pounding my chest, and singing songs of rejoicing. The dread of Day 2 and Day 3 still hung over me, but I celebrated like I had won a war.

And I had.

The mini panic attacks that I had getting up to do those speeches were the last that I had since. Something strange began to happen. Normalcy crept back into my approach to speaking. God healed me.

And I killed my fear.

When I finished the final speaking engagement, I walked to my car and I sat inside of it. I cried. A little at first and then more. It wasn't the tears that I'd shed mourning the loss, it was the joy that God put in its place. The Bible says that sorrow lasts for the night, and joy comes in the morning. I was in joy mode.

I want to allow you to dream again about an anxiety-free life. I promise you, I'm not special. Now, hear me out. I don't mean that God didn't make me intricately. In that regard, I believe I'm special. But, with respect to the choices, the weapons, and the battle, you have as much access to these resources as I do.

God revealed one final thing to me after I had my last panic attack. He told me why He permitted me to go through this to begin with.

The Real Purpose Of It All

Like any preacher that loves a good story, I get so tempted to relish the fact that David won and that he killed Goliath. I get so excited to scream from the rooftops that the Giant is dead and that God's purpose in putting David there was to win the battle and to conquer in faith.

But if I do that, I forget the rest of the story. The bigger picture.

After David killed Goliath, let's examine what happened above the Valley of Elah.

> "And the *men of Israel and Judah rose* with a
> shout and pursued the Philistines as far
> as Gath and the gates of Ekron, so that
> the wounded Philistines fell on the way
> from Shaaraim as far as Gath and Ekron."

— 1 Samuel 17:52, ESV, emphasis mine

There are two things that happened concurrently. First, we see the men of Israel and Judah rose with a shout! This is different than the crew that stood at an impasse, afraid to approach this evil creature. This is a much different picture than that painted of Saul expressing the inability to win against Goliath.

This was an emboldened group of people. Why? Well, that's rather elementary. Because someone was able to do something that they thought they couldn't do. Now, once that road was paved, the nation of Israel walked on it.

The second thing that happened, the Philistines fled. They ran. This is very interesting to me, and I think it's worth examining. This godless army pinned their hopes to a giant who would fight their battle for them, but once he was out of commission, they were out of courage. But there's a greater thing going on in this revelation.

They ran from the armies of Israel.

Here's what I believe. I believe Israel had the ability to defeat the Philistines the whole time. I believe they just didn't know it. And they needed someone to remind them that God would give victory and that they simply needed to trust him.

This battle went on forty days too long. God already gave them everything that they needed to win the fight against their enemies and to take the territory. But there was Goliath. He was big to them, but puny to God. And it took someone who was puny to them but big to God to kill the giant that was killing them with fear.

That's how God works, isn't it?

> "But God chose what is foolish in the world to shame the wise; God chose what is weak in the world to shame the strong."
>
> — 1 Corinthians 1:27, ESV

What happens when a fool does something in faith? They become wise. And they shame conventional wisdom.

Staying in ministry with constant panic attacks was the most foolish thing I had ever done in an earthly sense. But I know now why that was. I know why God made me go into the valley of Elah. I know why I made so many mistakes in dealing with fear (trust me, I'm not David, Matt Chandler).

I was put through that for you.

I was put through that to be a voice to you in the sleepless night reminding you of the faithfulness of our God.

I faced pain and got low so you could rise.

I was put there to embolden those that are sitting staring at the valley.

I wasn't put there for me, I was put there for you.

There is nothing between you and killing your fear. God has already given you the victory in Christ. God has already promised you healing in Christ. God has already gone ahead and given you the battle in Christ. Living in fear isn't just living in fear of what would happen if you move forward, but it's living in a way that is inconsistent with the way God designed you to live.

It's not to shame you, it's to empower you. I don't want you to be discouraged. I want you to be angry. I want you to be sick of it more that sick from it. I want you to change your outlook from that of a worrier to that of a warrior. You can't get into the valley and kill your fear if you sit on the side and pray that it will just go away. You have to run with the victory you know that God wants you to have.

The Place Of Dread Becomes A Memorial Of Deliverance

The weekend after I delivered my final keynote, I was standing in the secret place, looking up at the stairwell where this nightmare began and thinking about the original nineteen steps.

Everything looked different. I didn't feel that dread. I didn't even feel panic.

Don't get me wrong, I was shakier than Ronald McDonald watching a Jillian Michaels video, but I felt something different than I did before when I preached. I felt *good.*

Something flooded my memory that I hadn't recalled once since entering my nine-month fear fight.

Dead center in the nineteen steps from the pulpit to the back room was a little space below the stage. When I first started attending the church, I realized that God wanted me to teach a Bible study. I met a small group, twelve to sixteen at most, and we met right in the front of the church. I had a little music stand that I set my Bible on. That was the first time I opened up the Bible to teach. It was a special place. A sacred place.

When I recalled that place as the place of my first exercise of that spiritual gift, I started to cry. It may sound cliché but the devil wanted me to forget a special place.

I reworked the conclusion of my sermon to incorporate that sacred place. I walked to the platform, nineteen steps, and the panic was gone.

It took every bit of my energy to not cry. Right in front of the whole church. I had never experienced such a relief. Such a joy. Such—

Victory.

The title of my sermon was called "God's Cure for Depression." And it was from Psalm 77. I had written the sermon years before, but it spoke to me now more than ever.

The conclusion that God gave me threw the camera people for a loop. I told them to follow me as I walked back the nineteen steps and stood in the middle of them. I stood in the corner. I made this proclamation to the church and it's the same proclamation I make to you here.

God wants to take your place of dread and turn it into a memorial of deliverance. You see, that little nineteen step journey, at first brought me delight. Then, I lost my perspective and for almost a year it was a place of dread. Now, it was a memorial of deliverance. A place that will always remind me of how good God is and how nothing, including fear, can cause Him to lose His goodness.

Or His power.

Let's see if David caught onto this idea.

> "And David took the head of the Philistine
>   and brought it to Jerusalem, but he put
>   his armor in his tent."
>
> — 1 Samuel 17:54, ESV

It's gross that David took Goliath's head, but necessary to prove that the giant was dead.

But I love the next part.

It says that David brought Goliath's armor to his own tent.

If you recall, the Bible described how formidable Goliath looked in that armor. The detail. Even the weight. The Israelites shuddered at the sight.

It was a vision of dread.

David turned that vision of dread into a memorial of deliverance.

Can I tell you that God wants that for you? I'm not saying if you have a fear of public speaking, that you should go become a public speaker. That might not be what you should do. I'm not saying you should do the thing that purposefully make you miserable.

I'm saying that for most of your life, you've had things that you believe God wanted you to do but you haven't and fear is the culprit. The Goliath-sized armor has become your visualization when it comes to your dream. And it's killing you slowly. It's sapping your joy. It's stealing your life. It's ruining your relationships.

Maybe, just maybe, God doesn't want you to use His strength to live with fear. Maybe, He wants you to use His strength, to kill your fear.

If you go through this with the mindset of the warrior, you'll end up with armor in your tent as well. Your very own memorial of deliverance.

AFTERWORD

VISUALIZE A FEAR-FREE LIFE

In October of 2017, I told the church my story. I did it through a series of sermons entitled, you guess it, *Kill My Fear*.

It was the most rewarding thing I ever did in ministry. God healed so many people through the encouragement of His work in my story and to be quite honest, I grew as a pastor. Craig Groeschel says that people admire your strengths, but they identify with your weaknesses.

I'm as weak as they come with regards to this subject. So the whole purpose of this was to start a conversation. And this is the conversation I want to end with.

God has more for you than a fearful life. He has so much more for you than that.

In my office, on my filing cabinet, I have a picture held there by a magnet. It was a picture of me speaking at the keynote event for the non-profits and it's written from the CEO. I don't think it is a coincidence that there is a pose of her holding up my hand as though I won a victory after a boxing match. Outwardly, I looked great. Inwardly, I probably looked like ten rounds post-Mike Tyson (yeah, him again).

I spoke to the non-profit group that day about staying on your trail and having a vision for your life. They were moved and I had a voice with them because I work for a non-profit group. We share some of the same pain points.

In corporate training, Dale Carnegie teaches that you have to have vision. A definition of vision is a picture of a future state that does not now exist. There's an exercise I take clients through where they visualize their lives at a future date and time having accomplished that which they have purposed to do.

Can you do something for me?

Can you visualize a fear-free life? Can you dream about it? Can you close your eyes and think of a version of you that isn't paralyzed by fear? Can you picture six months from now, going and doing that thing that you have been putting off doing?

Would you allow yourself to imagine having a night where you slept all the way through without waking up in a cold sweat? Can you picture yourself speaking to your spouse openly after having come through this rough patch? Can you picture yourself enjoying reading a book and having the mental space not to divert your attention to fear?

What would it be like if you had a day where you forgot to worry about panic attacks? How about a month? A year?

God delivered me from fear's grip so I can encourage you in your journey. The purpose of this book is to pass off the good that God has done.

I believe that this verse speaks most to why this happened to me.

> "Blessed be the God and Father of our Lord Jesus Christ, the Father of mercies and God of all comfort, who comforts us in all our affliction, so that we may be able to comfort those who are in any affliction, with the comfort with which we ourselves are comforted by God."
>
> — 2 Corinthians 1:3–4, ESV

This verse says that we are comforted by God when we are afflicted so that we can be a comfort to those who are afflicted at later times. But we first must receive that comfort.

I can say without a doubt that the time I spent grappling with anxiety was the closest I'd been to God in my life. I prayed like my life depended on it, because truthfully, I had no other way to live. It was all through God's strength. I longed for God's comfort and He showed up in ways that I never imagined. I don't look at those days with dread anymore. I look at them as spiritual growth points, and a way for God to keep me in check. A sober reminder of how much I need Him and how He is capable of more than one deliverance.

I don't know your story. I don't know what brought fear into your life. I don't know what your symptoms are and I don't know what medications you've explored. I can't speak to every individual situation. But I know that there are millions and millions of people who struggle daily with anxiety. I know that because I've spoken to them. I know that because I've seen them walk through it. I know because I'm not extraordinary, but I was delivered from the bondage of fear and what fear might do to me.

But one more time, just in case you forgot.

It was always about you. You're loved. Jesus died for you. You were slaves to sin and Jesus rescued you from bondage. You were a servant of death and Jesus rose again to kill death. I refuse to imagine that Jesus broke the chains that bound you to a lost eternity only for you to become fear's prisoner. I don't believe he freed you to imprison you again. I don't believe fear is an end game in God's design.

That, I will shout from the rooftops. That, I will proclaim to anyone who will hear.

I recognize that your journey might be different. But one thing I'd ask you to consider.

Perhaps instead of trying to be accommodating, you become an assassin. Perhaps you take more charge of what you can control. Perhaps, if you were willing to read this, you're willing to go a step further, and believe in yourself and God enough to know that there is something more for you.

I am for you, I promise. And so is God. There is more than one way to kill your fear, but we have to kill it. We have to end it. We have to lay aside the familiar blanket of anxiety, and embrace a life that God truly has for you.

That's my prayer for you. That's my hope for you. And that's the dream.

This road is not going to be easy, but nothing worth anything is easy. You will be tempted to give up on that vision, but please, whatever you do, don't give up on your life. Don't give up on the vision of a different life.

A life where fear has no power.

A life where your future has no limit.

A life where God is displayed to others by what you do.

A life where fear is dead and you are more fully alive than you have ever been.

ATTACK PANIC BACK

You and I both know that panic attacks suck. I spent a lot of time in *Kill My Fear* talking about how to deal with fear in general. But for those of you who struggle with Panic Attacks like I did, I prepared something special.

If you simply sign up to my mailing list, I'll deliver you a free copy of my guide *Attack Panic Back*. It's a survival guide to your next panic attack.

I have no intention of spamming you. I will however let you know if I have anything else coming that you may find helpful for your battles with fear, or any other battles you may be facing.

Follow this address to get it.

https://www.subscribepage.com/attackpanicback

CAN YOU HELP ME?

If you've read this book, it means the world to me. I've prayed for you and I'm hoping you found my words helpful and empowering.

I'm an independently published author, which means I depend a great deal on positive reviews instead of depending on a large marketing budget (I'm working on it, okay!).

Could you please spare five minutes to review Kill My Fear on my book page. You can get to the page by going to the address below.

Thank you so much!

Follow the link below to review:
https://www.amazon.com/dp/B0858YYVBJ

ACKNOWLEDGMENTS

I am super grateful to some people that have been rock stars through everything.

First, I'm thankful for my wife, Jamie for letting me find my way through fear, and who remained waiting on the other side to celebrate with me. Also, I'm glad she didn't divorce me when I was lost in my own head.

Next, I'm thankful for both of my wonderful kids, Evie and Levi. So much of what I do is with them in mind. Healing was a priority because of them.

Finally, the church. I love you, Log Church. I've learned way more from you than you ever will from me. I am grateful to be your pastor. And I'm even more grateful that we have the kind of church that can be authentic enough to get real about anxiety.

With regard to the book itself, I'm thankful for the creative input of some of my staff. Specifically,

I'm most thankful for Stephanie Wertz. She read pieces of this at a time, then all of it, then more pieces. Then she read it again. Pray for her.

For Devan Gestrich, who took the concepts of the book and did a ton of design work early on. She's always up for a challenge.

And finally, thanks to Stuart Bache for your awesome cover skills and Josiah Davis for your editing team. Thank you for working with me!

SUMMARY, SCRIPTURES, AND QUESTIONS

ONLY TWO CHOICES SUMMARY

My Story

I'm a pastor of a large church and out of the blue, I had a panic attack right before administering baptism. I messed the service up, and started having panic attacks every time I spoke publicly. The battle with anxiety also caused me to bail out last minute from giving a toast at one of my closest friend's weddings.

God spoke to me (not in a creepy way that you might think) and told me I couldn't do anything (like leaving the ministry, or shifting my responsibilities) for at least a year. He also said that I must accept any speaking opportunity that I'm given.

Bummer.

Application

There's a lot to learn about anxiety, but the first thing is that you only have two choices in dealing with it. The first choice is to learn to live with it (most people select this choice, develop phobias, read books about coping, etc.). The second choice is to face it with the intention of killing it, and thus eliminating it from your life permanently.

Eeezy Peezy Lemon Squeezy.

Bible

> "And there came out from the camp of the Philistines a champion named Goliath of Gath, whose height was six cubits and a span. He had a helmet of bronze on his head, and he was armed with a coat of mail, and the weight of the coat was five thousand shekels of bronze."
>
> — 1 Samuel 17:4–5, ESV

> "When Saul and all Israel heard those words of the Philistine, they were dismayed and greatly afraid."

— 1 Samuel 17:11, ESV

"When the Philistine arose and came and drew near to meet David, David *ran quickly toward* the battle line to meet the Philistine."

— 1 Samuel 17:48, ESV, emphasis mine

"...fear has to do with punishment, and whoever fears has not been perfected in love."

— 1 John 4:18, ESV

"*There is no fear in love, but perfect love casts out fear.* For fear has to do with punishment, and whoever fears has not been perfected in love."

— 1 John 4:18, ESV, emphasis mine

Think About It

1. How long has fear been keeping you from living the life you wanted to live?
2. What would a life free of fear and anxiety

look like? Can you visualize it? Maybe jot some notes down to help.
3. What event triggered your anxiety?
4. When you think of the idea of running toward what you fear, what comes to mind?
5. The origin of fear seems overwhelming, especially if you are not a regular reader of the Bible. Do you feel confident in what will happen when you die? Have you trusted in Christ to take away your sin? If not, read for further reference: John 3:16-18, Romans 5:8, Romans 6:23, Romans 10:9-10, 2 Corinthians 5:17.

KNOW YOUR ENEMY SUMMARY

My Story

Having never dealt with panic attacks and general anxiety before, I sought answers in science and the Scriptures. I also realized that some of the ways I had been thinking contributed to my panic. Counseling, Scripture, and focus on my thoughts helped me to start to see some of the repeated patterns of anxiety's attack.

Cool beans.

Application

You have to recognize the tools fear is employing to keep you trapped in a state of anxiety. The greatest hits are three. First, fear forces you to play by its rules. Another thing that fear does is that it constantly forces you to listen to bad music. Your thoughts are killing you, but if we drill down, we will find it's the same thought repeated on a loop. Finally, fear masquerades as some of the other heavy hitters: depression, anger and hopelessness. At first glance, you might think that these things are isolated, but really, what we see here is that fear is dressing up for the job it wants.

Fear, you're so dumb.

Bible

> "Rejoice in the Lord always; again I will say, rejoice. Let your reasonableness be known to everyone. The Lord is at hand; do not be anxious about anything, but in everything by prayer and supplication with thanksgiving let your requests be made known to God. And the peace of God, which surpasses all understanding, will guard your hearts and your minds in Christ Jesus. Finally, brothers, whatever is true, whatever is honorable, whatever is just, whatever is pure, whatever is lovely, whatever is commendable, if there is any excellence, if there is anything

worthy of praise, think about these things."

— Philippians 4:4–8, ESV

"Then, at break of day, the king arose and went in haste to the den of lions. As he came near to the den where Daniel was, he cried out in a tone of anguish. The king declared to Daniel, "O Daniel, servant of the living God, has your God, whom you serve continually, been able to deliver you from the lions?" Then Daniel said to the king, "O king, live forever! My God sent his angel and shut the lions' mouths, and they have not harmed me, because I was found blameless before him; and also before you, O king, I have done no harm.""

— Daniel 6:19–22, ESV, emphasis mine

"And he withdrew from them about a stone's throw, and knelt down and prayed, saying, "Father, if you are willing, remove this cup from me. Nevertheless, not my will, but yours, be done." And there appeared to him an angel from heaven, strengthening him. And being in agony he prayed more earnestly; and his sweat became like great drops of blood falling down to the ground."

— Luke 22:41–44, ESV

"He stood and shouted to the ranks of Israel...Choose a man for yourselves, and let him come down to me."

— 1 Samuel 17:8, ESV, emphasis mine

"When [they] heard these words of the Philistine, they were dismayed and greatly afraid."

— 1 Samuel 17:11, ESV

"For forty days the Philistine came forward and took his stand, morning and evening."

— 1 Samuel 17:16, ESV

"...behold, the champion...Goliath by name... spoke the same words as before. And David heard him."

— 1 Samuel 17:23, ESV

"...Eliab's anger was kindled against David, and he said, "Why have you come down? And with whom have you left those few sheep in the wilderness? I know your presumption and the evil of your heart, for you have come down to see the battle.""

— 1 Samuel 17:28, ESV

"And Saul said to David, "You are not able to go against this Philistine to fight with him, for you are but a youth, and he has been a man of war from his youth.""

— 1 Samuel 17:33, ESV

"...Goliath of Gath, whose height was [9 feet, 9 inches]. He had a helmet of bronze on his head, and he was armed with a coat of mail, and the weight of the coat was [126 pounds]. And he had bronze armor on his legs, and a javelin of bronze slung between his shoulders. The shaft of his spear was like a weaver's beam, and his spear's head weighed [15 pounds]."

— 1 Samuel 17:4-7, ESV

"And his shield-bearer went before him."

— 1 Samuel 17:7, ESV

Think About It

1. What are your thoughts like? What are your patterns like? If you wrote them down, would you be afraid to show someone? This may be fear's bad song.
2. What is something you could do right now to make yourself feel a little better? For me, it was exercise and going to a bookstore. What fills your material joy bucket and what could you do to take a commercial break?
3. What unreasonable terms has fear set in your life?
4. What phrase or phrases repeat in your mind when you are at the height of anxiety?
5. Are there any other negative things (depression, rage, hopelessness) that you have been dealing with? Are you sure it's not just fear dressed up?

MURDER WEAPONS SUMMARY

My Story

God impressed on me that this was going to last a year, in a sense. Knowing that, I began to dig into tactics that I could adopt to turn my defense into an offense. Panic attacks were still happening, and I was far from okay, but I began to recognize that fear was weak, and I was stronger.

Good stuff.

Application

Fear isn't going to leave you. You have to do what you can to evict it. Dare I say, kill it?

There are several things that you can do. First, start an affirmation journal including truths about

God, past victories you've experienced, truths about you, promises to claim, and finally things your grateful for. This helps you prime the pump of offense. More importantly, getting this stuff on paper provides FOCUS. Focus is to anxiety as garlic is to a vampire. So don't be afraid to get stanky with affirmation.

While you're at it, really get to the bottom of your What If. There's a good chance that the thing you fear is more advertised with the same amount of grandeur as Fyre Festival was (please Google this, but wait until you're done reading this book because you're going to want to watch the documentary).

Lastly, less talky about fear and from fear while adding more talky from you. Use your voice to channel truth and put fear on the run, even though it's not getting away alive. We are in it to win it, friends. And fear is about to get capped.

Fear, you're toast.

Bible

> "But David said to Saul, "Your servant used to keep sheep for his father. And when there came a lion, or a bear, and took a lamb from the flock, I went after him and struck him and delivered it out of his mouth. And if he arose against me, I

caught him by his beard and struck him and killed him. Your servant has struck down both lions and bears, and this uncircumcised Philistine shall be like one of them, for he has defied the armies of the living God.'"

— 1 SAMUEL 17:34–36, ESV

"For God gave us a spirit not of fear but of power and love and self-control."

— 2 TIMOTHY 1:7, ESV

"There is no fear in love, but perfect love casts out fear. For fear has to do with punishment, and whoever fears has not been perfected in love."

— 1 JOHN 4:18, ESV

"For the gifts and the calling of God are irrevocable."

— ROMANS 11:29, ESV

"Give thanks in all circumstances; for this is the will of God in Christ Jesus for you."

— 1 Thessalonians 5:18, ESV

"...The Philistine said to David, 'Come to me, and *I will* give your flesh to the birds of the air and to the beasts of the field.'"

— 1 Samuel 17:43–44, ESV, emphasis mine

"...The Philistine said to David, 'Come to me, and I will give your flesh to the birds of the air and to the beasts of the field.'"

— 1 Samuel 17:43–44, ESV

"Then David said to the Philistine, 'You come to me with a sword and with a spear and with a javelin, but I come to you in the name of the Lord of hosts, the God of the armies of Israel, whom you have defied. This day the Lord will deliver you into my hand, and I will strike you down and cut off your head. And I will give the dead bodies of the host of the Philistines this day to the birds of the air and to the wild beasts of the earth, that all the earth may know that there is a God in Israel.

— 1 Samuel 17:45-46, ESV

Think About It

1. Is God telling you anything specific about your battle with fear? It's okay if He isn't, however, if He is, write it down.
2. What experiences have you had with journaling? What is something you can implement immediately to start an affirmation journal?
3. If you don't want to keep a journal, that's okay. But do me a favor. Answer the following questions here (you can write directly in the book or take notes on your e-reader).
4. What do I know of God that makes me want to stand up and shout?
5. What's one victory God allowed you to win in your life? If you would say none, I would suggest you think about the cross and the resurrection.
6. What is one cool thing about yourself that you know to be true?
7. Is there a Scripture that you've claimed on your life? Specifically, with regard to fear?
8. Name three things you're grateful for right now.
9. Take a walk down What If Avenue and

really examine how much truth is there. You may need to ask someone to help you with this. Sometimes an extra set of eyes on your thinking doesn't hurt

10. How do you describe your battle with anxiety? What can you say right now to fear to get it running away? I know you have something in you to say.

DEAL THE DEATH BLOW SUMMARY

My Story

As I approached speaking at a friend's church and keynoting an event, anxiety went all in. I doubled down and realized that I was coming up to the main event.

Spoiler Alert: I won. I preached. I spoke at the events. And I haven't had a panic attack since.

A+ ending. Five-Star Review, please.

Application

This might sound redundant, but you have to plan on running toward that which you fear. It's not going to go away. Planning to do the thing that causes your anxiety will get you closer to killing it. That's the first step: advance.

The second step is that you have to do this more than once. I know, it sucks. But here's the good news: once you realize you can survive, you can plow through to more and more victories. And fear will be utterly powerless to stop you.

R.I.P. Fear. You dead.

Bible

> "And David said, "The Lord who delivered me...will deliver me..."
>
> — 1 Samuel 17:37, ESV

> "...For the battle is the LORD's, and he will give you into our hand."
>
> — 1 Samuel 17:47, ESV

> "When the Philistine arose and came and drew near to meet David, *David ran quickly toward the battle line to meet the Philistine.*"
>
> — 1 Samuel 17:48, ESV, emphasis mine

> "And the *men of Israel and Judah rose* with a shout and pursued the Philistines as far as Gath and the gates of Ekron, so that the wounded Philistines fell on the way from Shaaraim as far as Gath and Ekron."
>
> — 1 Samuel 17:52, ESV, emphasis mine

> "But God chose what is foolish in the world to shame the wise; God chose what is weak in the world to shame the strong;"
>
> — 1 Corinthians 1:27, ESV

> "Blessed be the God and Father of our Lord Jesus Christ, the Father of mercies and God of all comfort, who comforts us in all our affliction, so that we may be able to comfort those who are in any affliction, with the comfort with which we ourselves are comforted by God."
>
> — 2 Corinthians 1:3–4, ESV

Think About It

1. What does moving toward fear look like for you?

2. Name something tangible right now that you can do to show fear that you're not letting it keep ground from you. Would you be willing to call someone and tell them what you're doing?
3. What is a place of deliverance for you? Somewhere sacred. Are you able to take a trip there and have a quiet time of reflection and prayer?
4. Write down five things that you'd like to see in your fear-free life. Be as specific as possible.
5. Think of one person that you know who is battling anxiety. Give them a copy of this book and tell them what to focus on. Don't hoard God's healing.

ABOUT SAM

Samuel Linton is a pastor from an awesome church in Pittsburgh, PA called The Log Church (http://logchurchpa.org). He's been there since 2004.

You can check out his online hub at https://www.samuellinton.com. You can also connect with him on Twitter @SamLintonWrites and Facebook at https://www.facebook.com/sam.linton.73.

Not only is Sam a pastor, he is also a fiction writer, a corporate business trainer, and lover of bookstores.

www.ingramcontent.com/pod-product-compliance
Lightning Source LLC
Chambersburg PA
CBHW070920030426
42336CB00014BA/2464